THE JAPANESE WAY *of* PARENTING

THE JAPANESE WAY *of* PARENTING

And What It Taught Me About Raising (Mostly) Calm, Caring, Capable Kids

Lisa Katayama

WORKMAN PUBLISHING • NEW YORK

Workman
Workman Publishing
Hachette Book Group, Inc.
1290 Avenue of the Americas
New York, NY 10104
workman.com

Workman is an imprint of Workman Publishing, a division of Hachette Book Group, Inc. The Workman name and logo are registered trademarks of Hachette Book Group, Inc.

Interior design by Remy Chwae
Cover design by Becky Terhune
Cover illustration by Saori Wago

Library of Congress Cataloging-in-Publication Data on file

ISBN 978-1-5235-3185-1 (paperback)
ISBN 978-1-5235-3187-5 (ebook)

First Edition March 2026

Printed in the United States (LSC) on responsibly sourced paper

Printing 1, 2026

Some names and identifying details have been changed to protect privacy.

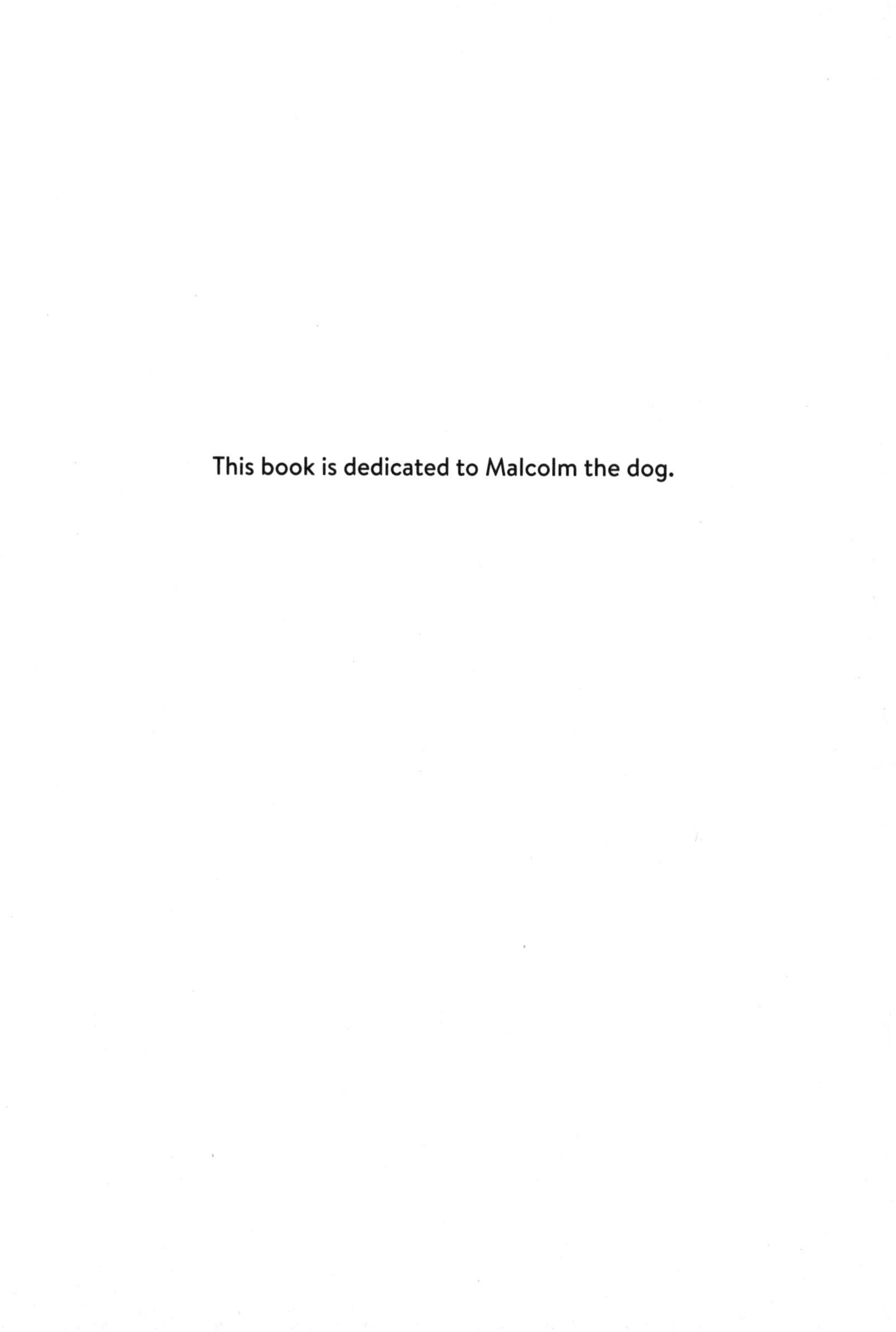

This book is dedicated to Malcolm the dog.

CONTENTS

ONE

Hello, Parenting. Goodbye, Me Time.

One of the hardest-hitting realities of becoming a parent has been the almost complete annihilation of me time. Gone are the days when a 90-minute candlelight yoga class was the only thing on my Sunday agenda. In my new reality as a full-time working mom of two small kids, I'm lucky if I can get a sip of my morning coffee, which Hubby diligently prepares for us every morning, before it gets cold. I wake up to a wailing baby and fall asleep while my resistant toddler negotiates to keep the lights on a few minutes longer so we can read another book or eat string cheese together. My back feels like it needs to be stretched out with a rolling pin because I bend over about a hundred times a day to pick up food morsels and stray colored pencils and tiny inside-out socks.

No matter how many things I pick up, more things end up on the floor minutes later. Adult conversations with Hubby have pretty much ceased; whenever we try to have one, we quickly get interrupted by enthusiastic chatter about rainbows and unicorns, or urgent calls for help coming from the kids' room.

In those rare moments when I do catch my breath, I end up thinking about the kids anyway. I scroll through pictures of them on my phone. I look for fun activities we can do together—pottery classes, toddler-friendly theater shows, a new park to explore. I think about interactions I had with them that day and ask myself, Am I showing up the way I want to for them? How can I be a better parent, guide, and friend in the phase they are in now? How can I bring more calm, controlled energy into difficult moments? How can I raise my children so that they are happy, safe, and successful at what they do and how they choose to live?

I have two daughters, N and M. They're almost exactly three years apart in age. So far, they seem to really like each other and we're having a good time building our rapport as a family.

Hubby and I are from very different cultural backgrounds, and our kids are mixed race; America would label them as Black and Asian. Being in a multicultural family is not new to me. I was born and raised by a Japanese dad and a Chinese mom and spent my formative years in a small international community in Tokyo, where most of my friends, like me, spoke a mishmash of different languages at home. Growing up, I spent the holidays in Hawaii with my mom's free-spirited hula-dancing sister and her Jewish yogi husband. I always felt a little bit like an outsider growing up in Tokyo with my foreigner vibes and multiracial friend group, but not in a bad way—I feel like I got many of the benefits of a Japanese childhood without being bound to the rigid societal rules and expectations. I haven't lived in my native land since I was eighteen, but I've stayed connected over the years through frequent visits back home to see my family and friends.

I put off motherhood for a long time. In my twenties and thirties, as some of my closest friends were hauling toddlers around while simultaneously navigating their first jobs or getting their PhDs, I had the great fortune of being responsible mostly only for myself. After college, I worked as a freelance journalist in San Francisco, then held a series of program leadership and consulting jobs in some of the most innovative spaces in the world, from the storied MIT Media Lab in Cambridge to research centers in Nairobi and Mexico City to the headquarters of iconic global companies like Nike, Starbucks, and Google. In my spare time (I don't even know what that is anymore), I volunteered at an AIDS hospice, hung out at the local climbing gym, and explored fun, offbeat Bay Area events like Bay to Breakers and Burning Man. In my late thirties I met Hubby, and shortly after that, I became a mom.

In those final few precious years before I had kids, I lived in the trendy Dogpatch neighborhood of San Francisco with my two dogs, Ruby and Malcolm. On most days I woke up peacefully on my own, walked sleepily over to the neighborhood Philz Coffee where the barista would make my pour over coffee by hand, and then chit-chatted with neighbors before biking along the waterfront to my designer office where I'd have my real breakfast, a granola-and-fruit smoothie made with a little communal bullet blender, before my day officially started. When I got home,

I had tea and ice cream before bed, by myself on the couch. I had the great privilege of having pockets of pure boredom—something I now know I will not have again for at least another decade, until my kids are teenagers and don't want to hang out with me anymore.

When I became pregnant with N, many of my closest friends pointed to my stellar track record as a dog mom as a reference point for how I would be as a human mom. "I know motherhood will come naturally to you," my childhood friend Lara said. "You've been the best mommy to your fur babies for years and years." One of my besties, Lindsay, wrote, "Motherhood: So far, so good!" in large letters in my baby shower book, next to photos of my two dogs looking deeply smug and satisfied.

As it turns out, being N and M's human mom is nothing like being a dog mom. Ruby is no longer with us, but Malcolm is, and he is by far the easiest kid in our household. He does not rush me through my morning coffee. He does not command me to walk across the house a million times to get things for him. He does not force me to talk to him in a slow, steady tone while ignoring everything I say, testing the outermost limits of my patience. He does not have meltdowns, and he does not scream at random intervals. His childcare does not cost thousands of dollars a month. He doesn't co-opt all my weekends with extracurricular dog activities or smear shea butter and Sharpie pen markings all over the living room couch.

Obviously, having kids means adopting a completely new lifestyle.

But it's not just that.

Having kids has made me take on a completely new identity myself.

For some reason, around the time when I became a parent, I also found myself wanting to be closer to my Japanese roots. I'm not exactly sure what triggered its onset. Maybe it's a side effect of being at the precipice of official middle age. Maybe the global pandemic and political tensions of the 2020s are taking a toll on me, triggering a subconscious need to be closer to my roots. It could also be that my mixed marriage is making certain cultural differences feel more pronounced. Hubby is of West African origins, and while our cultures have some similarities—like our proximity to the ocean, the belief in ancestral spirits, and our love of curries and stews—they are also on opposite ends of the spectrum on some very fundamental levels. In West Africa, where Hubby was born, people love to have heated debates, but the Japanese almost never openly argue with one another, even if they silently disagree. We also have a completely flipped sense of time. In Japan, meetings start as soon as the second hand on the clock hits the designated time; where Hubby comes from, a meeting starts only when everybody arrives, which could be hours later or even the next day. When I say two minutes, I literally mean 120 seconds; when Hubby says two minutes, it could mean anywhere from five minutes to an hour. There are upsides to having a partner with a polar opposite framework for almost everything, but it also gives rise to a deep sense of homesickness.

But I think the number one reason for my sudden Japaneseness is the fact that I'm now on the hook for raising responsible, respectable human beings who will one day navigate the universe on their own—and I think, of everything I've known so far, the Japanese culture is one of the best in the world for developing that responsibility and respect.

Here in the San Francisco Bay Area, it's not uncommon at all to have families with diverse cultural backgrounds. There are many different modalities you can use to raise children: gentle, conscious, free-range, child-led, snowplow, RIE, lighthouse (I won't get into each of them, but if you're a parent yourself you may have done some research into at least some of these). Hubby and I have chosen to raise our daughters in a Japanese-inspired environment in the United States. N and M go to a Japanese immersion school. They speak Japanese with their teachers and school friends. They spend extended time with family in Japan during their summer break. They take off their shoes when they enter any indoor space and love eating rice and natto (gooey fermented soybeans, an acquired taste for most non-natives). Our Spotify playlist has many of the typical kids' songs, like "Twinkle, Twinkle, Little Star" and the soundtracks to *Frozen* and *Moana*, but they prefer to listen to them in Japanese. Their stuffies have the names and likenesses of iconic characters like Pikachu, Anpanman, and Hello Kitty.

As I watch these two tiny humans who came out of my body learn about the world around them, I find myself wanting to nurture and provide for them in the same ways that the society around me nurtured and provided for me, all those years ago on the other side of the planet. Things like:

- Respect and reverence for the people and things in our community. Japanese society is rooted in the concept of omotenashi—radically caring for others. If everybody treats one another with extra care and consideration, harmony ripples through society.

- Routines and rituals designed to nourish the body, mind, and spirit. The Japanese say itadakimasu (bon appétit) before meals and gochisousama (thank you for the feast) after they finish. They take off their shoes before they walk into any indoor space. They take baths every night. They stay connected to nature and communally celebrate the changing colors of leaves and the first bloom of the cherry blossom tree.

- Calm, clean, simple, well-designed living. A well-designed life is both a pleasing aesthetic and a functional necessity. We keep our spaces clean and our things organized for our own peace of mind and for that of everyone around us.

- Healthy food options and sensible eating habits. In Japan, 7-Elevens offer a variety of dinner options, from ready-to-eat rice bowls to bento boxes with multiple colorful, nutritious dishes in one easy-to-carry container. Anyone anywhere can get a balanced meal for under ten dollars.

As I stumble through the mazelike universe of parenting, I want my kids to understand how interconnected we are with our surroundings and to know how to be respectful of others while still being themselves. I want them to have a baseline understanding of what neat and organized looks like. I want them to feel empowered to do things on their own, like putting away toys or preparing their own snacks. And I want them to see that learning to carry their own weight is part and parcel of being committed to the greater good. How can I provide some of this experience to my kids, even though we don't live in Japan?

Japan is known for its many inventions. The Sony Walkman. The flat-screen TV. Toyota. Honda. Subaru. Video games. The first humanoid robot. A high-speed rail system that inspired the world—and gave birth to a subculture of densha otaku, hardcore train enthusiasts who collect train memorabilia and travel to remote places just to ride on certain railway lines. Most of the anime and manga on the global market. Sushi, ramen, and the most Michelin stars in the world. Judo, karate, and aikido. LED technology. Zen philosophy and the chicken pox vaccine. Street fashion that inspires global fashion trends. The Japanese are also responsible for the inventions of the plastic umbrella (before this, umbrellas were made of cloth), the electric rice cooker—and, of course, the emoji, which is actually a Japanese word that means "picture letter."

Until the 1868 Meiji Restoration, Japan was largely closed off from the rest of the world. It was only after the feudal system (if you have no clue what I'm talking about, watch the Hulu smash hit TV series *Shōgun*) was abolished that it started to become the modern industrialized nation it is today. In the decades that followed, the Japanese built shipyards and mills, developed commerce pipelines and adopted Western technologies, and started building its now-famous train system and communication lines. Castles were turned into military control centers. Buddhist temples and Shinto shrines were shut down. The Empire of Japan was born—and along with it, many of the cultural characteristics of today, like a strong work ethic and commitment to collective progress. Japan also made some suboptimal choices that culminated in its siding with the wrong side of history in World War II, hurting many people and communities along the way. When Japan and the Axis Powers lost the war, Americans temporarily took over the country, rewrote the constitution, and imported cultural ideas like modern love and democracy to Japan in a comprehensive reform effort. Japan committed to recovery and redemption, and built a new economy with values updated to match modern times. What exists today is a result of this historic context, plus a mishmash of other influences that streamed in over the last few decades, resulting in the Japanese culture of today that is admired by so many.

Why is the same country that spawned Pokémon, Street Fighter, and the Prius responsible for some of the most courteous and well-behaved humans on the planet? To get to the answer, you have to look at the kids.

In 2022, Netflix rereleased a nineties Japanese TV show called *Old Enough!* The premise is simple: Parents from all over the country send very small children—some still in diapers—out into the streets to run household errands. In one episode, a three-year-old boy and his five-year-old sister take a boat and a train to a neighboring town to pick up dinner ingredients and cold medicine for their mom, who is under the weather. In another, a trio of toddlers sets out with a little tote bag and a thousand-yen bill to purchase firewood for a neighborhood barbecue. These are real kids and real parents navigating real daytime streets, monitored only by a couple of stealth cameramen disguised as construction workers to quietly film these precarious experiments. The subjects of this reality series exhibit an odd juxtaposition of behaviors: On one hand, they're typical toddlers, singing while they walk, getting distracted by puddles, dropping and forgetting things. But they also have a strong sense of duty to complete the mission they were assigned to do and a curiously mature-for-their-age situational awareness of how to behave in public. Even though they've been on this planet for only a few years, they seem to have a tacit understanding of the role they are meant to play.

Old Enough! was an instant hit on Netflix. Aside from being hilariously cute, the show also triggers the type of head-shaking disbelief that hooks people. Who in their right minds would send their precious underage offspring into the scary public streets alone? Don't these crazy parents worry about car accidents or abduction?

The simple answer is, not really. This might seem irrational and irresponsible, but these daredevil adventures are on brand with Japanese-style parental love in action. One of the very first values that parents teach their kids is how to respectfully and seamlessly hold their own in an interdependent society. It's our moral duty to equip our little ones—even if they're less than three feet tall—to be responsible participants in this ecosystem who can follow instructions, not cause trouble, and blend into society. And since all of society is helping to support the safety and well-being of its young people, we parents don't have to dedicate all our time and energy and every nerve in our nervous system to making sure our offspring are fed, nurtured, educated, and safe. When the built environment is designed to be more accommodating for its littlest citizens, then we can unleash our offspring into the wild earlier and more often.

This belief is a strong part of my own family's history, too. My dad, who is Japanese, lived on his own from when he was just a kid. He grew up in a seaside town in southern Japan with his parents and two siblings, where the family owned and operated a small bamboo craft store on a modest shopping street near the ocean. When he was thirteen, he and his fourteen-year-old brother boarded a train and moved to Tokyo on their own to attend middle school in the big city. They lived alone, but despite their freedom, they didn't veer off their destined path. My dad stayed in Tokyo for university and then moved to Colorado for grad school, where he met my mom. He became a businessman, while his older brother worked as a researcher at Georgetown University in Washington, DC. By all measures, their parents' commitment to getting the boys a better education that would lead them to a new life path seemed to work.

And this isn't just a "long time ago" story, either. My nephew's fourteen-year-old friend Shinzo recently moved from Tokyo to Nagoya, some four hours away by car, to attend a prestigious high school where he received a basketball scholarship. He's living on his own, in an apartment complex that includes meal service. "I'm mostly just excited," he says when asked how he feels about it. "The only thing I worry about is whether I can keep my space clean. I'm going to be busy with studying and basketball." I've known Shinzo for a few years; he came to stay with my family one summer to attend a basketball camp in the Bay Area. While he was here, he always picked up after himself, never left stray socks or shoes in the home, always spoke in quiet and polite Japanese to me, and still had a great time.

In Japan, independence isn't about individual achievement or standing out from the crowd; it's about doing your part in a society that works together, rather than pulling away from existing norms. To nurture this type of independence, kids are taught from an early age to do things on their own. "My kids have been commuting to and from school by themselves since they were six," one mom tells me. "Then they take themselves to their after-school activities. If they get hungry, they buy snacks at the convenience store with their cell phones." This experience—small single-digit-aged kids taking themselves to and from school and appointments—is so common that I am hard-pressed to find a Japanese family in Japan that doesn't think this is okay. In some neighborhoods, there are restaurants that feature special menus designed for latchkey kids who want to have a nutritious meal on their way home from school.

There's a solid, science-backed reason why parents might want to allow even the littlest kids a bit of contained independence. Children who are given some unsupervised time are more likely to develop a sense of autonomy and personal responsibility. They learn how to solve problems on their own, which helps them develop important tools for adulthood like executive functioning, socio-emotional learning, confidence, and resilience. America's struggle with overparenting has been well documented and critiqued from all over the world. "It's ironic that in a country so committed to freedom, children have so little of it; that in a society so committed to personal responsibility and self-reliance, children can do so little for themselves," writes Stephanie H. Murray in *The Atlantic*. Many scientific studies have linked overparenting with depression and anxiety. And yet, in America, many kids are basically shackled to their parents until they turn eighteen, at which point they're suddenly on their own without any real-world experience. At a toddler swimming class at our local YMCA in California, I observe a very enthusiastic dad, whose three-year-old boy happens to be in the same little pod as N, repeating every single instruction that the swim teacher gives his son. The teacher—a soft-spoken young man whom I suspect is a college student trying to make a few extra bucks doing this as a summer job—says to the kid, "It's your turn."

As soon as the words leave the instructor's mouth, the dad yells, "Buddy, it's your turn!"

"We're going to practice kicks," the teacher says.

"It's time to kick, buddy!" the dad yells. "You got this, bud. Kick your legs. Arms out."

Why does this dad feel the need to repeat everything the teacher is saying? I wonder.

At a sprawling park in an upscale neighborhood not far from where we live, I observe a huge flock of families gathered around a play structure. The sound of kids playing is overpowered by the loud voices of their micromanage-y parents. "No no no no, Jack! Slides are for going down, not up!" "Where is your brother?" "Honey, here, hold my hand. You can't climb that by yourself!" Nearly every child has a hovering guardian nearby. I feel like if I don't watch my toddler's every move, I'll probably look like a bad parent, so I unenthusiastically follow my kid around up and down the colorful stairs and baby slides. There are as many adults walking around these giant play structures as there are children. As we pass one another on the playground equipment (Why am I even on this playground equipment?), some of the parents give me understanding half smiles, as if to say, "Isn't parenting so crazy—but fun?" (It is, I think, while I return a fake, grimace-like grin, but I don't need to be hanging from monkey bars to find my joy in this moment.)

Hubby and I spend so many hours every week shuttling our kids back and forth from home to school to playdates to ballet classes, picking up after them, cooking for them, reminding them to do basic things, that I can't imagine having to do this for another decade and a half, until M is eighteen. There's only one clear way out: the Japanese way. I need to teach them to be more autonomous, safely and within reason, so that I'm not their servant for life.

I'm curious if three-year-old N can responsibly do some shopping on my behalf like the toddlers in *Old Enough!*, so I invite her to come with me to our neighborhood grocery store. (If I sent her out alone, I'd probably get arrested.) "N," I say calmly. "We're going to the store to get three things: a cucumber, eggs, and cheese. Okay?"

"Okay!" she yells, excited about the new responsibility. She opens the fridge and helps herself to a vanilla cupcake, licking off the frosting before plopping the rest of the cupcake on the table.

"Do you want to walk, drive, or take the stroller?" I ask her.

"I don't want to walk," she whines as she pulls her black slip-on Nikes on the wrong feet. "I want stroller."

"Okay, let's take the stroller," I concede. We live at the end of a cul-de-sac, next to a church, and although it's a very quiet neighborhood, it can be busy with cars and there isn't always a sidewalk. We walk past the usual array of East Bay houses—Edwardians and Tudors and mid-century moderns with front lawns full of native plants and succulents. N is happily swinging her legs and singing a Japanese song about blowing bubbles that she learned at school. "The bubbles flew to the roof, they flew to the roof, and then popped and disappeared," she sings while we stroll past a scary pumpkin scarecrow sitting on a wooden swing (it's mid-October—almost Halloween), half a dozen plastic skeletons, and a semi-deflated Pikachu balloon that she demands we stop and stare at for about three silent minutes before she instructs me to keep strolling.

We finally arrive at the store. "Do you remember what we're getting?"

"Ummmm . . . juice!"

"No, not juice. A cucumber, eggs, and cheese," I remind her. She walks confidently down the aisle, her little braided pigtails bouncing against her unicorn t-shirt. She arrives at the butcher counter.

"Can I have a sticker?" she asks the butcher, who happily complies. "We need butter," she tells me. I remind her of the cucumber, which she snatches up along with an ear of corn. She then speed-walks toward the refrigerators at the far end of the organic veggie aisle in search of butter.

"Don't get lost!" I yell, almost too quickly, even though we are in the safest grocery store in all of the East Bay.

N navigates the twists and turns of the narrow store aisles like a pro. It reminds me of many of the Japanese kids featured in *Old Enough!*, who similarly walk around as if they know exactly what they're doing. She must feel proud that I've given her a mission, a responsibility that I normally take on myself. She gets briefly distracted by some lollipops displayed in a corner, but I counter-distract her by pointing in the opposite direction, toward the cheese section. A questionable move on my part because N loves cheese, maybe even more than she loves lollipops. She starts grabbing whatever is within arm's reach and dropping it into my basket: "circle" cheese (her word for Babybel), string cheese, a block of sharp cheddar cheese. The snack aisle is an especially arduous part of the journey, but somehow, we make it through without adding too much more sugar to our purchase.

One hundred forty-five dollars and forty-eight minutes later, we're leaving the store with five kinds of cheese, four energy bars, a cucumber, an ear of corn, a watermelon, a container of marinated octopus, and a dozen eggs. By the time we get home, a bright orange sunset is peeking out from behind the nearby cemetery. "It's so fun together, riiiiight?" N says as she unloads the stroller, making exaggerated "Umph!" and "Yoisho!" (which means "umph!" in Japanese) sounds as she lifts heavy items up the stairs and into our foyer. She insists on doing this task by herself. "I can help you," she says. "I'll get some muscles!" My kid wasn't as autonomous or mission-focused as the kids in *Old Enough!*, but I can now see how—if she was provided with a combination of safe environment, societal expectation, and trust—she could potentially achieve a level of self-sufficiency that would be accepted by Japanese society.

Parenting is hard; there is no one-size-fits-all solution to how to do it right. Those of us raising our kids in the United States have a constant rotation of unprecedented challenges, like school shootings, the increasing cost of childcare, and political divides unlike anything we've seen before. Like most modern parents, I am determined to customize my parenting adventure. With so many competing theories on how to raise kids, it's honestly impossible to wrap our heads around everything. Modern science is teaching us more about a child's brain than we've ever known before. And yet, the vanguard is ever changing, and there is no right answer.

So how do we choose what works best for us?

In exploring my own answer to this question, I've stumbled into a model of Japanese-inspired parenting in America that I think even non-Japanese families can benefit from. And that's what led me to write this book. This book centers around the story of me raising my kids, but I also offer up some simple tools and takeaways based on some foundational values of Japanese culture that I believe anyone can use as they develop their own theories about raising children in an increasingly customizable world.

This book covers roughly six years of my family's life, from my first pregnancy with N, to her early years as a toddler, to M joining us three years later. Writing it took some solid research and observation, a lot of fun conversations with friends and experts, and some deep personal reflection. I researched different theories of parenting and their origins. I spoke to other parents and subject matter experts, who expanded my perspective on the practices and methods unique to Japan and on parenting in general. I did some deep introspective work into how I was raised, and how that impacts who I am and how I am raising my own kids. My kids are still little and there are still a lot of unknowns, but I'm excited to share how I've brought Japanese parenting practices and principles into these early years, and how it's setting the foundation for the long and winding parenting path that inevitably stands before me.

TWO

It Takes a Village

I'm sitting on Bus #01 from Shibuya to Roppongi, a popular public transportation route that takes the people of Tokyo across a busy six-lane artery called Route 246. It's a wet and humid weekday at the beginning of the city's infamous rainy season, and after dodging tourists and puddles on the ten-minute walk to the bus stop, I'm relieved to be dry and in motion. I board at the front, pay my fare, and make my way toward the middle of the bus. It's 4:30 p.m., the beginning of rush hour. A little boy who is maybe seven years old is reading a novel on the window side of a two-seater. He doesn't look up as I approach him; instead, he politely moves his tiny blue umbrella a bit closer to his side of the bench, a subtle signal that I am welcome to take a seat. His lunch bag is already neatly positioned on his lap, under the novel. When I look around me, I see at least four other kids in a similar age range, on their way home from school. I wouldn't have noticed them if I hadn't been looking because they're not making any noise or causing any trouble—like everybody else on the bus, they're quietly, respectfully making their way to their desired destination.

I melt into my seat and gaze out the window, enjoying my last few minutes before I pick up N at her summer preschool and go into parent mode again. I have an evening full of toddler negotiations and diaper changes ahead of me. But this moment? It is mine and mine only. I'm relishing it, sitting quietly, reflecting. This city in which I was born and raised is truly the biggest, cleanest, coolest place in the world, I think, as the bus whizzes through town. In some ways, it's like any other major city. It has buses, cars, office buildings, government buildings, residential neighborhoods, working people, nonworking people, gangsters, a police force, and lots of retail shops. The buildings and highways are stacked vertically and horizontally, a Chutes and Ladders–like maze of never-ending concrete designed for efficiency and functionality. This is the city structure that inspired movies like *Godzilla*, *Tokyo Drift*, and *Lost in Translation*. Fourteen million people live in the city of Tokyo, speed-walking through massive ant tunnel–like train station systems and shooting up and down the quietest high-speed elevators in the world. Even as the media is buzzing with news of the declining yen, the local economy feels robust and efficient. Restaurants are packed, people are shopping, the roads are full of activity.

Despite the density of the city, there is almost no chaos, no trash on the streets (there are no trash cans, for that matter; people are expected to take their own trash home), not a dust bunny in sight no matter what restaurant or shop you walk into. There are no loud noises. Even emergency vehicles wail at a palatable volume, unlike the anxiety-inducing screeches of the American fire engine. There are no potholes on the roads; if one is found, a construction worker is sure to be fixing it the next morning. The sidewalks teem with millions of businesspeople and blue-collar workers who keep the city functioning, and the tourists and shoppers, and the hyperlocal grandmas and grandpas who have lived here all their lives. Walking among them are little kids, humans less than four feet tall, walking to school with their boxy Randoseru backpacks, fiddling with their train passes and chatting quietly with friends, while salarymen in stiff suits rush past them in their signature staccato rhythm. Shuffle shuffle shuffle rush rush rush. All over the country, little underaged commuters take themselves to and from school using public transportation.

I look up from this train of thought and see that this bus has gone from mostly empty to fully packed with commuters. The vibe has shifted but the noise level has not changed. A middle school boy with a black backpack, a matching black bag, and shiny black shoes is standing at the front of the bus doing long division in the air with his tiny fingers. His mouth moves silently: *five hundred and thirty over sixty-two, five hundred ninety-eight over eighty-two.* After each math problem, with a barely visible satisfied nod, he pencils the answer into a small box in the corner of his worksheet. He shuffles off the bus at the next stop and, without looking up, continues doing his long division as he trudges down the sidewalk.

The kids on the bus are the young seedlings of the society of Japan, which operates like one giant living, breathing organism. Their perfect behavior—not taking up too much space, not making too much noise, making sure not to disrupt the flow of things around them—is not an anomaly. These are the fruits of the very intentional collective labor of the country, a rigorous training aimed at designing a highly functional, peaceful society. When you train an entire country to be this way, you can expect—with some certainty—that the world it spawns will function as a synchronized whole.

Omotenashi—radically caring for our surroundings and for other people—is one of the most important values of Japanese culture. At the 2022 World Cup soccer tournament in Qatar, while other countries' fans were spraying beer on one another and leaving popcorn on the floor, Japanese fans went viral on social media because they were seen picking up trash—their own, but also that left behind by fans from other countries. "For Japanese people, this is just a normal thing to do," Hajime Moriyasu, the coach of the Japanese Football Association team Samurai Blue, told *The New York Times*. "When you leave a place, you have to leave it cleaner than it was before." The fans weren't the only ones who brought these deeply ingrained cultural habits to Ahmad bin Ali Stadium. The soccer players themselves left their changing room spotless, again prompting amazement across social media. In many other parts of the world, when people attend a festival or a sports game, they just trash the place, believing that it is not their job to clean up their own mess. Maybe someone is hired to clean it up. Maybe not. The Japanese don't think this way. They whipped out their own trash bags and went aisle to aisle picking up other people's used paper cups and candy wrappers. The rest of the world watched this in awe, but if you're familiar with the culture, this comes as no surprise. These fans, after all, are the grown-up versions of the kids on the bus, trained from an early age to respect their surroundings and pick up after themselves and not cause trouble. When a massive earthquake devastated the Tohoku region, causing nearly 16,000 deaths and $220 billion in damage, the displaced residents didn't overtly complain, or get angry, or fight with one another. They lined up for food and shared what little they had. There was no disorder, no chaos, no looting. "There is no question the Japanese respond well to this kind of catastrophe, but even if it looks remarkable from the outside, it's not new," Carol Gluck, a professor of modern Japanese history at Columbia University's Weatherhead East Asian Institute told ABC News at the time. "It's not cultural or religious. It is a historically created social morality based on a response to the community and social order."

Omotenashi literally means "no front or back." It's the reason that many of the things that are highly impersonal and often stressful in other parts of the world are really organized, systematic, and pleasant in Japan. You notice this from the moment you land in the country. At the airport baggage claim, there is a person whose job is to turn the bags coming down the conveyer belt so that the handle is facing out and the wheels are facing up, which makes them easier for people to pick up. The bathroom stalls are wide and have foldaway changing stools for people who want to change out of their airplane clothes without dropping them onto the dirty floor. As you leave the terminal, cabdrivers check the backseat to make sure you didn't forget anything before they shut the door. Walk through the doors of any restaurant, even the most bare-bones mom-and-pop diner, and you're greeted by an enthusiastic call of irasshaimase! (Welcome in!). If you go shopping on a rainy day, storekeepers encase paper shopping bags in water-repellent plastic, with holes cut out for the handles so you can hold it on your way home. Then, they carry the bag to the door for you after you make a purchase and stand at the entrance of their store, until you are out of sight, bowing every time you look back.

Having a little bit of omotenashi is innate in all humans, not just the Japanese. People are actually happier when they are kind to others. According to a 2017 study by Soyoung Park at the Center for Cognitive Neuroscience in Berlin, acts of kindness and generosity trigger activity in happiness-related areas of the brain. An audit of nearly thirty experiments, conducted by Dr. Oliver Curry, a University of Oxford anthropologist who serves as chief science officer of the nonprofit Kindness.org, found that people who were assigned to help other people were much happier than people who were assigned either to do nothing or to help only themselves.

"Humans are social animals; we've been living in groups for millions of years, and many ways of interacting with others are mutually beneficial," Dr. Curry tells me. "Getting along with other people is very valuable. So just like other valuable things in the world, we've evolved an appetite for them, and we've evolved various intuitive motivations and guidelines to make the most of social life." Whether that's helping members of our family, working in teams, buying gifts, or sharing resources, he says, "we have discovered ways of unlocking the benefits of a whole range of cooperative opportunities."

In a CNN special, Anderson Cooper spends time at the "baby lab" at Yale University, where researchers have found that morality is innate in kids—it's not something that parents teach. Using puppets, the team shows simple examples of good and bad behavior to a six month old—the green bunny helps a tiger open a box, while the orange bunny sabotages the effort by slamming the box shut. Later, when the baby is presented with the orange and green bunnies, she immediately hugs the green bunny. "They gravitate toward the helpful characters and the friendly characters from very early on," says Dr. Karen Wynn, who runs the lab. "When [babies] look at a social interaction between two individuals, they can tell whether that's a positive one or a negative one—and they're drawn towards the positive character." Eighty percent of the time, the babies in the Yale study chose the green bunny. The big takeaway? Babies are not taught the difference between good and bad, right or wrong; they're born knowing it.

The Japanese are famously punctual. Everyone is always on time, all the time. When the schedule says a train is arriving at 4:23, it arrives at 4:23. (And if it's running even one minute late, the stationmaster goes on the loudspeaker and offers sincere apologies for the inconvenience it causes commuters. Can you imagine if the MTA had to do this every time a New York City subway was running one minute late?) When a party invitation says the event starts at 8:00 p.m., people line up outside the door at 7:55. Zoom calls with my Japanese colleagues always start exactly on time—people typically join one to two minutes early to make sure they aren't the last person there. If you join a video call exactly on time, you'll see that there are already multiple people on the call (unlike US-based video calls, where I'm often met with the automated response "You're in the call but you're the first one here.") Lateness is the ultimate infraction, a sign of disrespect and the thing that tips the orderly society off-kilter.

Whenever a Japanese person goes on vacation or a business trip, they always come back with something for everyone else. Japanese people are always stopping at gift shops no matter where they go, always thinking about what to bring home to their spouse, kids, coworkers, and maybe even the person who brings them their mail or their dry cleaning. The practice of gift giving, or omiyage, is often prefaced with words like tsumaranai mono desuga . . . which means "This is such a boring thing, but . . ." This signals that you are offering the gift with humility and that your taste would never live up to their expectations. We often say things are kimochi dake—just representative of the feeling (of gratitude, of congratulations, of camaraderie, of happiness, whatever that particular moment of gift-giving might symbolize). The art of Japanese gift-giving is not to be mistaken with gift registries for weddings, baby showers, and other special occasions. "It's incomprehensible to me that you'd ask someone else to buy you daily use, practical things," a Japanese friend says to me with a mildly shocked tone. "It defeats the purpose of omiyage." Omiyage is not supposed to be practical. It's supposed to feel like what Americans think of as a hug—a warm, delightful moment of connection.

American vulnerability guru Brené Brown says that trust isn't built in grand gestures but in small moments of caring. Japan is meticulously constructed with tiny cinder blocks of caring at literally every corner, bolstered by the determination by all citizens—no matter where they're from, how old they are, or what their ideologies might be—to believe wholeheartedly that taking care of those around you is just as important as taking care of yourself.

In the 1990 classic *Etiquette Guide to Japan: Know the Rules that Make the Difference!*, the late Japan beat journalist Boyé Lafayette De Mente observed, "Japanese people could anticipate one another's attitudes and reactions to the point that verbal communication was often unnecessary." He's right: Japanese expressions are subtle. We are not a culture of big hugs or I love yous or I miss yous. We can say more with a simple expressionless nod than what most Americans say in a mouthful of words. When a Japanese person finishes a meal, they put their chopsticks back on the chopstick holder, facing the right direction. They fold their napkin and place it on the right side of the table. They push their chair in straight before they leave and say gochisousama deshita (thank you for this meal) with a slight nod even if nobody is listening.

Tokyo is one of the safest cities in the world because if you radically care for others, you won't steal or drive too fast or vandalize other people's things. Most people leave their bikes and strollers unlocked on the sidewalk all day, all the time, sometimes with their handbag still in it, and nothing gets stolen. If you lose your wallet, it will most likely get returned the next day, cash intact. Pretty much every driver on the street follows the rules, and even if there were the occasional rule breakers, it wouldn't be a problem because nobody jaywalks. When everyone is cosigning on the same behavioral contract, as long as this keeps getting enforced, we can all exist within a bubble of safety. It's kind of intense. But it works.

In the book *The Hidden Life of Trees*, German forest scientist Peter Wohlleben talks about the lyrical interdependence of the living beings in a forest, and it reminds me a lot of the beauty and intensity of Japanese society. "An organism that is too greedy and takes too much without giving anything in return destroys what it needs for life," he writes. Japanese society is like that, too—an interdependent, network-like ecosystem. Children are an important part of that network—tiny trees that need to stand on their own to keep the forest's ecosystem functional and sustainable. This sense of moral responsibility begins at a very early age, especially in the public eye, and is reinforced every step of the way by the government, by the adults in their lives, and through lots of peer pressure. The reinforcers are all around us, and for the most part, they take on a gentle if not slightly passive-aggressive nature. They take the shape of hundreds of signs, handwritten, typed, printed, that instruct people on how to behave, what to watch out for, what not to do. Often, public instructions are narrated out loud by a robotic lady voice that warns you to watch your step as you get on or off the bus, to hold on to a strap or pole as the vehicle departs, to not forget anything as you leave your seat. No matter where in the country you may be, robot lady is there to serve, equipped with a repertoire of polite recorded messages to the community so that every experience, whether you're about to hop onto a moving walkway or step into a supermarket, feels carefully guided.

For a long time, what makes a good Japanese child was not a suggestion or a subjective truth. Here's my version of it, extracted from my own observations plus the types of things I've seen kids get in trouble for not doing:

A good Japanese child . . .

- listens to their parents and teachers
- know what's safe and what's not
- is never too loud in public
- says "thank you" and "sorry" often, at the right times

- does not jaywalk
- does not run indoors
- does not run outdoors unless in a setting designed specifically for running
- does not make a mess
- is considerate of other people's needs and feelings
- always keeps the peace and never causes meiwaku.

Meiwaku—causing trouble for others—is the cardinal sin of Japanese society. It's a word that small children become intimately familiar with and that follows them throughout their lives. Any act or phenomenon that causes a deviation from the precisely expected norm is considered meiwaku. "Don't stand up from your seat," I observe one mom tell her son on the Ginza line subway. "It is meiwaku to the people around you." "Don't talk so loudly," a dad warns his daughter in a soba restaurant near my parents' house. "It is meiwaku to the other guests." "If your daughter continues to whisper to you during the performance," an usher explains to me during intermission at a performance of the musical *Frozen* at a theater in Tokyo, "it will cause meiwaku to the other viewers, and we may need you to move to the satellite viewing room." (Side note: Isn't it amazing that they have a satellite viewing room for noisy kids?) "Don't *ever* be like that person," a man who catches me jaywalking says loudly to his kid, so I can hear. His message is actually for me, the adult child who never learned this important lesson, whose digressive behavior is a huge heap of meiwaku to everyone around me, even though technically I'm not putting anyone other than myself at risk. The kid nods in quiet agreement.

Japanese children know that top-notch behavior is part of their moral duty as a citizen of society. Being a good Japanese kid is not an easy job. It's not supposed to be. This societal system works only if everyone in it believes that the greater good of the community is more important than individual happiness. This entire nation was built on putting other people first.

On a recent visit back home to Tokyo, I had coffee with my friend Lulu, who unleashes her eight-year-old daughter, Kimi, into the wild on a single-speed bicycle with a little wicker basket to get to and from after-school tennis lessons with a little flip phone hanging from a string on her neck. "She can only call three people on that thing," Lulu laughs, "me, my husband, and my mom." Being a good Japanese child is about pulling your own weight. Kimi is a good Japanese child because, by being capable of commuting by herself, she frees up her mom to spend her afternoons getting a workout in or catching up with friends at her favorite café. In Japan, the chances that a small child will be subject to accidents or crimes are so incredibly low, and kids are trained at such a young age to not wander off, that almost every parent feels perfectly at ease with their kids walking around town without their constant supervision.

Japanese parents hardly ever brag about our own kids. Being good at something or naturally gifted in any superlative way isn't considered the ultimate goal. In general, it's better to just get along with others and not stand out than to be exceptional. The objective of Japanese parenting isn't to raise the best, the brightest, the most unique. Kids don't need to be prodigies or geniuses. The early years of life are really about learning how to get along with others and develop a caring nature that helps them navigate situations with cool calmness and decorum. When we compliment other kids, it's often using phrases like "He's such a shikkarimono!" (He's got a good head on his shoulders) or "She is a dekiruko" (She is a capable child).

My nephew Shota is a good Japanese child because he doesn't ever make a scene in public, and he always considers other people's safety and well-being. When he was three, I took him to a playground across the street from his grandparents' house, where half a dozen kids were doing a circuit on a giant metallic slide. Shota waited patiently until he was at the front of the line, slid down with a huge smile, and started to make his way back up the hill for another turn. Then, he saw a girl slightly smaller than him coming down the slide, so he quickly reversed direction and squatted at the bottom of the slide with his arms reaching out in a protective stance to make sure she didn't fall. ("What a shikkarimono he is!" a mom witnessing this small gesture said, to which I replied with humility, "Oh, it's nothing.") Shota has been taking himself to and from basketball practice across the city on his bicycle since age eight. This frees up his dad to do business dinners without having to worry about childcare.

When my second kid, M, was born prematurely at thirty-three weeks' gestation, my parents hopped on a plane from Tokyo to San Francisco to help us with N and do the daily NICU circuit with Hubby and me. It was an amazingly special, sacred time where we all got to participate in nurturing our tiny little child next to her hospital incubator until she was ready to come home and be with the family. The day M came home from the hospital, we all sat on the couch in our living room as the tiny infant was gently passed around from grandparent to grandparent. She was mostly sleeping, but every so often she would squeeze someone's finger or open one eye and turn the side of her little mouth up into a subtle grin. "Orikousan ne!" my mom squealed in delight, which means "What a well-behaved child you are!" It was an interesting choice of words, given that the baby was not even six pounds and wasn't technically behaving like anything. But then again, if you subscribe to the idea that it is a baby's responsibility as a citizen to begin life with human connection, like squeezing fingers and smiling, this makes a lot more sense. When you look underneath the hood of Japanese culture and what makes it work, it's easy to see why the independent children of *Old Enough!* aren't just a gimmick, but the result of a society full of orikousan.

Japanese culture is far from ideal. By staying so committed to its fixed ideas of what society should be, the country has birthed some of the world's most courteous, hardworking people—and, has inadvertently designed a system that is deeply resistant to change. Today's Japan is knee-deep in managing the side effects of a society built on outdated ideals, like gender bias and age-based discrimination, neither of which are inspiring young people to follow in the footsteps of their parents and grandparents. They're resisting the well-trodden path by making radical decisions, like not working for companies and rejecting the pressure to get married and have babies by a certain age. This is putting the entire nation of Japan into a bit of an existential stupor. The resilient cultural norms that have withstood global wars and recessions may not survive this next wave of change. As comedian Trevor Noah observed on his podcast *What Now? With Trevor Noah*, "On the one hand, I think it's beautiful that Japan has this idea of rules and following them, and everybody has to do the right thing. But there's a downside to it, right? . . . One of the overarching questions I found Japan kept on making me ask is, At what point should you bend to accommodate others? And at what point do you say that no, no, this is who I am or this is who we are and this is the way that we're going to stay?"

Despite its imperfections, there are valuable ideas we can take away from how children are raised in Japan that are useful to anyone—no matter where they live. The Japanese are famous for their resilience, kindness, and ability to stay calm in the face of adversity. During the COVID pandemic, we learned that we can't survive by watching out for just ourselves. A harmonious response and consideration for the greater good of the whole community were some of the underlying values that helped Japan stay relatively safe while other countries struggled. Instilling these values in our young people just might be the key to spreading more of that calmness everywhere—an antidote to the rising tensions and uncertainties of the modern world.

THREE

Mini Japan in Big America

Getting a child into the right day care in the San Francisco Bay Area is like trying to catch a rare Pokémon. Even though babies are too little to care what they do with their lives, their parents—tech executives, doctors, artists (sometimes all in one insanely ambitious human)—are, more often than not, competitive, meticulous, and obsessed with their kids' futures. New parents are expected to apply for their children's day care months before they are even born to secure a spot at some of the top schools. This is a microsociety in which survival of the fittest takes on a whole new meaning.

N was born at the height of the 2020 COVID pandemic, when schools and day care centers were on lockdown. Nobody was leaving home, never mind touring germ-infested shared facilities. And yet, when I start searching for a day care situation for N several months after she's born, I am already behind. Nearly every place I reach out to tells me I have to be on a wait list.

In the San Francisco Bay Area, the education options are vast. Let's say you want your kid to speak French. You can pick from a bilingual school that caters to wealthy families from the nation of France; a day care filled with the kids of people from Francophone colonized nations; or the Lycée Français in the center of the city. There are several Chinese immersion schools—one that is a public school, another that is private, another that teaches both Chinese and Japanese to babies as young as eighteen months. I come across at least half a dozen day cares that teach Spanish and English, but I also find one that teaches Spanish and Japanese, and yet another that teaches Spanish and French.

With all these options, I try to focus on the things that matter most to me. Here are a few of them:

Who will her friends be? I firmly believe that the first friends you make shape your framework of friendship, one that you carry with you for the rest of your life. I grew up in a small international community in Tokyo, where I hung out with the same ten kids from age five to fifteen, and I can confidently say that many of my best and worst traits were either developed in tandem with or in response to my relationship with these kids. The place where N makes her first friends could be the place where she finds her lifelong best friends. It's also the environment in which she will learn how to handle the emotions that invariably surface in toddler life: jealousy, fear, loneliness, and uncontrollable joy—among many others. Ideally, she will experience all these ups and downs in an emotionally safe environment with clear boundaries and a solid set of role models.

Who will my friends be? As one of those extroverted introvert people, I'm very picky about who I spend time with. Early in my career, in the mid-aughts, I knew many people in the tech and tech-adjacent industries in San Francisco. I had tons of people in my network and was constantly running in circles trying to keep up with dinner parties and coffee dates. Some of these people I loved and continue to love today, but at some point, I realized I had too many people in my life and that social time was getting in the way of other things that were important to me. In an attempt to pare down my crowd, I made three lists: people who gave me energy, people who took my energy, and people with whom I had no choice but to spend time (this included relatives, coworkers, and questionable partners of close friends). Then, I took everyone on the second list and deleted their numbers from my phone.

By the time I'm embarking on my day care search, I'm in my forties, and I feel pretty good about my close-knit circle of friends and family. I'm not about to resurrect that second list, not even on behalf of my beloved tiny daughter. I've heard the nightmare stories from other moms about the types of banal conversations they're subjected to at playdates and birthday parties. Social osmosis is no joke.

What kind of environment will she be in all day? Having grown up in Tokyo, my expectations of my lived environment are sky high. I am sitting in a coffee shop in San Francisco writing this sentence right now, and in my immediate vicinity I see—and am bothered by—chipped paint on the wall of the café, cracked pavement where my car is parked, and seven garbage cans. You can imagine how particular I would be about the look and feel of the place where my child will spend forty hours a week. I want her to know what it feels like to be in a clean and beautiful environment all day—and to not have to numb herself to the chaos of an unkempt space. We parents take huge leaps of faith by leaving our kids with virtual strangers all day. It will comfort me to know that my kid is in a serene space with chill people who have the mental and psychic bandwidth to care for her without being distracted by a chaotic environment.

What kind of behaviors will she bring home? I am not a paragon of good behavior. I was kind of a rebel when I was a kid. To my mother's horror, I sometimes spat on the street and peed in the shower. When we were teenagers, my friends and I spent hours playing video games in Shibuya and partied on the streets of Roppongi until the break of dawn. As a college student home for summer break, I kept a strict schedule of coming home at 5:00 a.m., sleeping until 3:00 p.m., waking up to repeat the same thing over again. I'm not sure how my parents let me get away with it, but they must have kept me in check in other ways because I turned out all right in the end. I think. I still keep up the resistance in little micro-moments, even as one of the primary adults in a four-person household. Last night, Hubby reprimanded my daughter for eating broccolini straight from the serving bowl with her fingers—something she most certainly copied from me. Sometimes I don't brush my teeth before bed if I'm really tired. Sometimes when Hubby's not home, I sneak my dog into bed, even though I know Hubby doesn't like it. I stuff my face into Malcolm's tiny adorable face and breathe in the faint cookie-like smell he emits when he's asleep, and it knocks me out like a strong dose of melatonin.

I think it's okay to be a rebel, but it's not what I want my kid to learn at school. I want school to be the place where she learns how to be an upstanding citizen of the world. Hubby and I are from two completely different parts of the world, but we're both Gen Xers, and many of our foundational cultural values are somewhat similar. We are ambitious and hardworking and a little bit angst-driven. We are both from historically patriarchal cultures. Despite our progressive worldviews, we believe in good manners and predictable behavior as a path to a more harmonious society. At a fundamental level, we feel that Japanese-style manners and behaviors can only help our little mixed-race daughter navigate life happily and safely, especially in a world that is going through a lot of ups and downs. Of course, I aspire for her to be her fullest and greatest self—I'm not a tiger mom!—but I do think having good boundaries and limits is just as important as good art supplies and outdoor space. My biggest failure indicator would be if she ends up as one of those entitled, spoiled, opinionated kids who talks back to her parents and refuses to do anything unless she really wants to do it. (In retrospect, I realize that every child has both moments of upstanding citizenry and unbridled entitlement. But the naive, new-parent version of myself did not know this yet.)

As parents and guardians of little ones, we have the incredible opportunity and responsibility to build worlds for our children that become the foundation of their entire existence on this earth. It's up to us how we mix and match the elements that are in it—daily activities and cultural elements, but also intangibles like the sense of safety, how they see and understand the world, and how they get along with others. Whatever we create and model becomes their baseline for the rest of their lives.

My mind is filled with these thoughts as I drag my confused husband to day care center after day care center within a five-mile radius of our home, which sits at the top of a scenic hill that spans several cities and counties of varying degrees of poshness. Our neighborhood still boasts a strong immigrant community, and as a result, the day care centers there are like a World Expo of childcare services.

For the first two years of her cute little life, N has a wonderful nanny from Tibet who comes over in the morning, takes her to a park nearby, and runs a makeshift day care with her nanny friends before bringing N back in the late afternoon fed, entertained, and passed out in her car seat. On rainy days they go to Barnes & Noble and read books on the floor of the children's section; for Losar, the Tibetan New Year, she dresses N up in a beautiful traditional robe and takes her to the temple for prayers and festivities. It's a system that works well while Hubby and I both work at home because of the COVID pandemic, but we hope the pandemic will end sooner than later—and we can't keep paying nanny prices forever, either.

At one day care center, three elderly women watch over half a dozen small kids sitting on a faded blanket in a dilapidated play space behind the head teacher's home. One kid stares at us from a potty in the corner of the playground, where he sits the entire duration of our visit—about half an hour. The next place we visit is run by a joyful woman in a long flowy skirt who welcomes us with buoyant energy, but her ceiling is covered with dozens of fluorescent hanging monkeys that make me wonder how in the world you can nurture calm kids in such a neon environment. (Maybe calmness is not the goal of this place, and that's okay. It's just not for me.) We visit another place that occupies a giant churchlike building and teaches its curriculum all in Spanish. And in a large multi-unit yellow town house down the street that takes up half a block, a school director in tight jeans and a slick black ponytail, who pulls up in a shiny Tesla ten minutes late, takes us upstairs to her very spacious office that overlooks the Golden Gate Bridge and gives us an intense pitch about the measurable academic outcomes of the children under her care.

Like any good, ambitious parent, I arrive at each destination with my laundry list of questions. How soon do we need to apply? Do you provide lunch? What do the kids eat for snacks? How do you get the kids to fall asleep at the same time? There's a place that serves homemade lentil soup for lunch, a place that plays Italian opera to cue naptime, a place with half a dozen baby photos taped to the window to show newcomers how long the wait list already is. Everyone seems to have their own unique take on how to nurture kids, and we listen with earnest awe and wonder to each spiel, asking ourselves if we can see our little N thriving there.

And then, one day, the three of us visit CB. Tucked away at the end of a steep cherrywood staircase behind the teacher's home on a busy hilltop commuter street, CB has no signage or obvious evidence of children. There are no toys in the front yard or stray toddler clothes (or toddlers) anywhere in sight. Hubby and I look at each other curiously as we make our way down a set of side steps to this mysterious space. Faint giggles and light footsteps invite us gently into the premises.

An unassuming dark-haired woman in a navy-blue cotton mask and a denim apron greets us at the wooden door. She introduces herself as Sensei, the patron saint of this establishment. As we round the corner, we see that the giggles and footsteps belong to six small children who look at us wide-eyed and wave as we enter their field of vision. N is at that golden age where she's emerging from babyhood into early toddlerhood, starting to vocalize and make funny noises like "aye aye!," clapping on command, making lots of eye contact. She's generally a happy kid. On the day of our visit to this school she's wearing a little unicorn onesie and soft purple sock-shoes. She clings cautiously to her dad as we lift the latch on the gate and enter the school yard.

Half a dozen pairs of adorable eyes flicker from us to the teacher and back to us. As if on cue, Sensei calls out to the kids in Japanese. "Everyone, a new baby is here to visit. Come say hello!" Immediately, all the kids turn from their respective activities.

A little girl emerges from the playhouse. A boy jumps off the geodesic play structure in the center of the yard. Two other kids walk over from the sandbox in the far corner. Sensei gestures for us to sit down on the rubber mat in the center of the playground. It's the height of COVID, so every kid is wearing a mask. Each of them, I notice, is wearing their mask properly so it's covering the nose and the mouth.

Maybe it was the pandemic isolation, or some residual postpartum loneliness, but this simple act of gathering almost brings me to tears. It reminds me of the type of synchronicity that I see only in my homeland, which the pandemic has kept me away from for three years and counting. The kids are not upset that they must drop what they are doing to listen to the teacher, and they all seem genuinely interested in meeting us.

N, who does not yet know how to crawl, props herself up on the playmat, leans tenderly on my right leg, and looks around curiously at her new environment. A little boy with sleek black boy-band hair leans in with the sweetest look on his face to connect with her and says, "Konnichiwa, boku Koji dayo." (Hello, my name is Koji.) The vibe is quiet, curious, sweet. Another little girl reaches out to touch N's toes gently.

"Everyone, you're a little close!" Sensei warns. In unison, every kid shifts back a few inches. I look at Hubby with awe. These kids are not just Japanese-style trained . . . they are Japanese-style COVID-trained! From this moment on, I am convinced that N must get into this school ASAP.

The East Bay of California is home to many sanctuary cities and as such has an incredibly diverse immigrant population. This region has birthed decades of historically significant activism and innovation: the free love movement, gay rights, the Black Panther Party, multiple tech booms. We live near the ocean, the mountains, the city. Our surroundings offer us a wide range of nature-based activities like camping and hiking and swimming in lakes while also immersing ourselves in diverse cultures—our cities celebrate Lunar New Year, Losar, Juneteenth, Cinco de Mayo, Ramadan, and Christmas. We get to take our kids trick-or-treating at homes decked out by artists who build for Pixar and Burning Man. In the midst of all this grit and dynamism and diversity, I have discovered a tiny little world that reminds me so much of home, a mini Japan in the middle of big America. Maybe I shouldn't be surprised, but I am—in the best of ways.

After our initial visit, I send Sensei a note:

> *It was so lovely to meet you, your staff, and your kids. We would love to apply for N to attend your school as soon as you are able to accept her.*

I end the email with a standard greeting in Japanese that you send to someone you hope to continue a relationship with. *Please accept my sincerest gratitude for your continued support*—and my name written in kanji.

Like every other school we visited, CB has a one-year-or-more waiting list. Sensei politely informs me that we are number three on the wait list for the fall semester of the following year. And so I wait patiently, praying to the Shinto gods that with some luck, being number three on the wait list will mean a guaranteed spot in this magical little world that I've just discovered.

The following spring, almost a year after our first visit to CB, we get the email we've been waiting for. A spot has opened up, and N will officially become a member of this little community starting at age two. I am overjoyed and relieved. Now I don't have to be the only adult in her life who is showing her the importance of shoeless interiors, polished manners and behaviors, saying "hai!" to authority figures, and eating multicolored, balanced plates of food.

I do have some concerns. The world likes to marvel at Japan's obsession with cleanliness, punctuality, and omotenashi, but it can also be an overly instructional, unforgiving environment. The Japanese are great at encouraging resilience and hard work, but they aren't as good at nurturing out-of-the-box thinking and emotional well-being, things I strongly believe all kids need. It's also questionable whether a Japanese upbringing sets people up for lifelong happiness; the country doesn't even rank in the top fifty in the World Happiness Report and has a higher-than-average suicide rate. Homogeneity—the art of not sticking out—is still a dominant character aspect of the culture; over 98 percent of the population is still ethnically Japanese. No matter how you slice it, my daughters—with their curly hair, brown skin, and African dad—will never blend in. Not that I want that, but . . . a part of me wonders how this Japanese foundation will affect my little mixed-race kids growing up in California. It's an experiment that could go horribly wrong—or mind-blowingly right.

On her first day of school, N wears tiny blue jeans, a little white sweater with red dots that vaguely resembles the Japanese flag, and a purple-and-yellow cotton face mask. She holds her dad's hand tentatively and lines up at the top of the wooden stairs that lead to the schoolyard. We've packed her a simple lunch: a little dinosaur-themed bento box with white rice, some chicken curry, and a little side compartment filled with peas and carrots. For the first couple of days, Sensei instructs us to pick her up early, right after lunch, to make sure she acclimates well before transitioning into the full-time program. In retrospect, this is a thoughtful and caring proposal, a way to keep the peace among all the kids as they welcome this new little one into their ecosystem.

At CB, Sensei runs a tight ship of repeated routines, creative play, and Japanese rituals and traditions. The same twelve kids, the same three teachers, spend every day in the same space, finding safety in consistency and learning how to find their own unique selves within this contained micro-environment driven by values like harmony, trust, and self-sufficiency. They line up to use the bathroom at the same time and eat their bento boxes in chairs perfectly spaced out across the most pristine classroom. They stare at katakana and hiragana (the ABCs of the Japanese language) charts all day. They plant seeds in the spring and harvest homegrown fruits and vegetables in the fall. They make beautiful lanterns out of papier-mâché and draw doodles on paper fans using sparkly Japanese gel pens. They play a version of red light, green light, but instead of screaming out the colors of the changing traffic light—stopping at a red light is a cardinal societal rule, not playground game fodder—they must freeze when the person counting says, "Darumasan ga koronda!" ("Mr. Daruma"—a symbol of good luck in Zen Buddhism—"has fallen down"), which is a much sweeter metaphor for the somewhat frantic game. They play kakurenbo—hide-and-seek—counting from one to ten melodiously in Japanese. They play freeze dance to Japanese folk songs and anime theme songs.

The kids start their day with an exercise routine sanctioned by Japan's national radio broadcast network. Have you ever watched elderly Asian people doing their morning stretches in a local park? It has that kind of vibe, but much more organized and codified. Back in Japan, every schoolkid, every blue-collar worker, every corporate person does the same exercise every morning, which entails some two-sided stretching, jumps, twirls, and swirls set to this bouncy tune. It's a great example of the uniformity that makes Japanese society so cohesive. By doing the same exercise with all your peers every morning, you bond, you level-set some shared health goals, and you boost morale. (Radio calisthenics, as it's called in English, was first invented in America, but the traction and stickiness and ubiquity of it is uniquely Japanese.) At the school's annual fall festival, each kid gets a book of tickets for the games (like scooping water balloons from a pool of water, fishing for plastic fish, and ring toss). Nobody gets more than one ticket per game—everyone gets one turn each, no exceptions. There are no winners or losers. As a result, there's very little bragging or fighting or taking more of anything.

While most Western parents are subjected to irritatingly catchy and meaningless kid pop tunes like "Baby Shark" and those on CoComelon, N is surrounded by a repertoire of classic Japanese folk songs about dragonflies, acorns, the ocean, and the voice of bugs. She sings about chestnut trees, feelings associated with the tea harvest, and other subtle connections among nature, childhood, and spirituality. About a hundred years ago, shortly after World War I, a team of musicians decided that children's songs needed to be more educational and connected to national interests. So they wrote a series of tunes called doyo, about flowers and birds and other nature-based themes that harken back to the nation's agrarian roots. Today, children's music in Japan has evolved to include more catchy tunes inspired by new manga and anime, but doyo still hold an important place in the lives of Japanese families and are often sung by parents and grandparents and teachers as a way to remind kids of the traditions and values that tie them to this country.

Like most toddlers, N doesn't yet know how to share, or wait her turn, or ask for what she needs. Instead, she will have a meltdown, screaming, "No, I don't want to!" But as she begins her journey at CB, something extraordinary happens: She learns how to be a member of a tribe, a small, well-structured community of toddlers who adhere to the routines and traditions of a Japanese-style hoikuen (day care center). By the time they're four, the kids are writing one another birthday cards in hiragana, saying owattara kashitene ("May I please borrow that toy when you are finished?") instead of grabbing for one another's toys, and saying itadakimasu! before every meal.

N's transformation is not unique. At Japanese immersion programs all over the world, little kids are learning to take off their shoes when they go in the classroom, to keep their voices down when they're indoors, and to clean up after themselves. Some schools, like CB, are independently run and put emphasis on values, language skills, and manners. Others layer language and culture immersion over other education philosophies like Montessori and Reggio Emilia. Others have been established by the Japanese government as satellite locations for expats to keep their kids up to speed with the education system in the motherland. Sarah Birke birthed her two kids in Tokyo while she was the bureau chief of *The Economist* there. When she moved to Mexico City a few years later, she chose to continue her kids' Japanese education by enrolling them in the local Japanese school created by the government for expats. "At my older daughter's school, they do everything pretty much the way it's done in Japan—the class meetings, the morning assemblies; they have their roles and assignments."

Some Japanese after-school programs focus more on keeping up with the Ministry of Education's curriculum. Others host all-day events in grassy fields with competitive games reminiscent of the sports days that take place in Japan. In an effort to preserve parts of the culture that would otherwise be lost in this country, a Japanese American church a few miles away from my house teaches traditional Bon Odori festival dancing to the descendants of people who were sent to internment camps during World War II.

Many parents of Japanese descent send their kids to immersion schools to teach the values and language of Japan. "My family lived through the internment camps in California," one CB mom tells me. "So they were taught to forget their heritage, to hide it. I want my kids to remember it again." Some families send their kids to regular public school but supplement that with a Saturday school called hoshuko, a super-intensive weekend program run by a network of nonprofits that aim to equip kids of all ages with a rigorous Japanese language and culture curriculum so that they could reintegrate into Japan's school system if and when they move back home. (Often you can identify adult hoshuko grads living in America by their polite, textbook-perfect Japanese.)

A lot of Japanese families living abroad try to spend the summers in Japan. There, the kids are immersed in the culture, the language, and the rituals. After a few months in the motherland, they're speaking crisper Japanese and are much better at following instructions.

"For us, it's a survival mechanism," one mom, who recently moved from Tokyo to San Jose, California, tells me. "Our family is in the US on a visa, and my husband works in an industry that has been seeing dramatic layoff rounds. At any point in time, it's possible that we'll have to return home, and when we do, if our kids are reading and writing at a first-grade level, but they're actually supposed to be in fifth grade, that'll be a problem."

It's not just the Japanese immigrants who seek this future for their kids. My ob-gyn as well as the doctor who actually delivered my baby—both of whom are ethnically Indian—send their kids to a Japanese immersion school nearby. At a rice paddy in northern Japan, we encounter a Caucasian family from California who tells us that their twin daughters, age five, speak fluent Japanese, even though the parents don't. "We wanted them to have a bilingual education," the dad, who is from Kentucky, says. "And we thought, Why not Japanese?"

CB is operated from a place of pure Japanese-style love. "I believe that love and discipline go hand in hand," Sensei tells me.

"Children need warmth, encouragement, and emotional security, but they also require clear boundaries to feel safe and develop self-regulation." She doesn't give out a lot of flowery language or praise. At the annual parent-teacher conference, Sensei gives N grades against a rubric that seems like a hybrid of American age-appropriate targets and some Japanese language milestones and explains to us what she does well and what she doesn't. At pickup, sometimes she says things like "N is putting in a big effort these days." But most of the time we parents hear about tactical challenges or receive constructive criticism, like this:

"Today at lunch Tako-chan refused to sit down with everybody, and instead took off his shoes and started running around the playground. Running barefoot is a safety hazard and also sets a bad example for other kids. Please talk to him about this behavior."

"Today N kept saying that her toe hurt, but we can't see anything wrong with it."

"Please make sure to pack lunches for N that don't make a mess. Her food got all over her shirt and the floor, and we had to clean up after her," she explains with a grave face. I apologize profusely and pack a different lunch the next day. It takes me a while to get it right, but I finally learn that smaller onigiri rice balls are better because they don't fall apart and that lunch boxes packed too full inevitably end up overflowing when kids clumsily go at it with their little spoons.

Sensei herself grew up with a traditional Japanese education that had a strong emphasis on values like respect, discipline, and collective responsibility. "My father was particularly strict about behavior and manners, and instilled in me the importance of politeness, kindness, and respect for others," she tells me. She started this school with a commitment to the structure and community that she found so helpful in her own childhood, but without the rigidity. "I strive to uphold these positive values—teaching good manners, kindness, responsibility, and respect—while incorporating more flexibility and opportunities for creative expression to support each child's individual needs." Sensei's style resonates with me. Despite her deadpan exterior, I can tell that she loves the kids a lot. On birthdays, she prints out photos of each child's year and makes colorful birthday books on neatly cut half-sheets of paper tied together with a ribbon, with messages from every teacher and child. And at the graduation ceremony—a child's final moment at CB—she reads out a heartfelt written speech about each graduating child.

Sensei's expressions of love remind me a bit of my own father. My dad, like many Japanese dads of his generation, doesn't openly show a lot of emotion, but I've never questioned whether he is a deeply feeling, empathetic person. I remember watching the Olympics with him one year, and glancing over at him as tears quietly rimmed his eyes as Japan won a gold medal. In my most challenging moments, my dad has always shown up for me, quietly and patiently, his words sparse but brimming with wisdom. For my baby shower, which took place on Zoom because it was in the middle of the COVID pandemic, my childhood best friend, Alyssa, collected messages from friends and family all over the world sending me well wishes for the arrival of my new baby. My dad sent in a photo of me as a four-year-old sitting on a swing while he stood proudly by my side and wrote, in Japanese, "I always wished for you to become a mama, but I didn't want to pressure you, so I kept that wish to myself. I couldn't be happier for you today." Japanese-style love is quiet, but sweet and thoughtful when it matters most, packing years of unspoken lovely feelings into a pithy statement.

Sensei adapts the Japanese way of raising kids to the Western ideals of freedom and self-determination. She teaches shudan seikatsu, which means that the students work together as a group and learn about their role in maintaining the whole, respecting others, and partaking in independent activities like cleaning up their meals and putting away toys in categorized boxes—all in service of maintaining a clean and organized environment. But she's also attuned to their individual needs and nuances and is pretty flexible about meeting each kid where they are—as long as it doesn't disturb the peace. It's this combination of loving acceptance and careful structure that seems to work so well for the kids in the school. "This blend allows children to experience the best of both cultures, developing discipline and cooperation while nurturing their individuality," she says.

As N begins her journey at CB, she starts to blossom more and more into herself—a bespoke combination of American, Japanese, African, and toddler that nobody could have invented if they'd tried. She pretends to play the piano while singing the ABC song with a Japanese accent. She strums the ukulele and sings Bob Marley while wearing Hello Kitty hair clips in her tiny Afro. She is unhealthily attached to her pacifier, which she calls Mamie—not to be confused with Mama, which is what she calls me. She runs various experiments, turning a remote control into a phone or cleaning my glasses with her wet wipes. She seems to have a penchant for fashion and design, placing her tiny shoes in a rainbow shape on the floor, taking the same-sized bite out of a dozen cherries picked from a nearby tree and placing the remainders in two symmetrical rows on a paper towel, or lining up a sticker sheet full of pandas in various poses along the windowsill so it looks like they're dancing. She puts together elaborate outfits using everyday objects like pool floaties and toy hats, and she likes to wear my only pair of leather high-heeled shoes and clomp around the house.

Before she turns four, N can cut along a straight line, pick up babies and dogs carefully and transport them across a room, and order her own food at a restaurant. She doesn't run off on her own, she cleans up after herself, and she can write her name in two languages. As time goes on, it becomes clear to me that her Japanese-inspired learning environment isn't turning her into a Japanese kid; it's just giving her another way to express herself and to explore the essence of who she is.

I reflect, rather gratefully, on the diligence and effort it takes on the part of everyone involved—the teachers, of course, but also the other parents in this tight-knit community—to reinforce these values of omotenashi, to teach the kids how to have kizukai (consideration) for others, and to make sure they do not cause too much meiwaku.

One day, we get invited to a little picnic hosted by a local Japanese family. The park is full of people from all walks of life—frisky teenagers, jumping elementary school kids, a multigenerational family reunion. The Japanese play group is perched on a set of four giant picnic mats neatly arranged in a giant square in the middle of the grassy lawn. As we approach them, a little girl without shoes on beckons to N from the mat. Hi, she says in Japanese while holding a rice cracker out toward N. Would you like a snack? Would you like to do some crafts? N instinctively takes off her shoes, lines them up right at the edge of the mat, and takes the girl's hand. In this chaotic park with wild children running all over the place, stepping into this picnic area is like taking a portal into another world. It's an oasis of Japanese-style peace and order. The older kids are helping the younger kids with their arts and crafts, offering to help them choose a color they like. N chooses purple, her favorite. Then they guide her to the decoration station, where there are scissors, glue, and a variety of papers and crayons. As more people arrive, the kids who are manning the picnic table go through the same routine—shoes off, a warm welcome, an offer of snacks, help with crafts. It's not like this group particularly stands out visually—in the broadest sense it's a bunch of toddlers bunched together and coalescing around shared play—but when you take a closer look, you notice that the cultural nuances and values that drive this play group are a little different. These kids are gentle with one another. They're kind, polite, communal. Shoes are lined up at the "entrance"—in this case, the edge of the picnic mat—facing outward so they're easy to put on when you leave. Snacks are packed neatly and organized, the kids are eating perfectly shaped onigiri rice balls with bonito flakes for lunch.

N's life at CB is filled with snapshot moments that show how she is slowly, steadily, happily becoming a more Japanese-inspired child. N with her hair in poofs holding an umbrella as she descends the stairs to school on a rainy day. N sitting on the school ground floor, surrounded by her classmates, attempting to eat hand-pounded mochi dipped in sweet chestnut paste made by her teachers with a pair of disposable wooden chopsticks as long as her torso. N in a candy-cane-striped summer dress, holding hands with her friends as they walk home down the tiny pathway to where we park our cars for pickup at a nearby cul-de-sac. N holding up a handmade star sprinkled with pink glitter that they made for the winter holidays. N holding hands with a little boy whose parents make the most beautiful Japanese-inspired colorful ceramic mugs. N considers ants and roly-polies to be her friends and has a keen understanding of the life cycle of plants and animals. She loves Hinamatsuri (the Japanese Girls Day festival) just as much as she loves Halloween; on both occasions, Sensei takes photos of her little mixed-race, mixed-age class, all 12 kids standing in a straight line and holding up artwork that celebrates each holiday, hina dolls cut out of paper plates for the former and pumpkins cut out of colorful foam sheets for the latter.

The CB community quickly becomes an important part of our family's day-to-day life. N and her friends play soccer together on the weekends. They all go to one another's birthday parties. Hubby sometimes gets drinks with the other dads, and I meet other moms for manicures and lunches. We celebrate holidays together, the Japanese ones as well as the more Western ones like Halloween and Thanksgiving. It's clear that the kids love and respect one another and that their social code operates on values like equity, peace, and harmony. We parents are the co-conspirators, the assistant producers of this collective adventure, working together with the kids, the school, and one another to create a culture that feels good to us, a generous dose of Japanese infusion in a tiny corner of this vast American landscape.

FOUR

Designing a Kid's Life the Japanese Way

As I settle into becoming a mom, I find myself obsessively organizing N's life. I fold all her tiny clothes neatly and then stash them in her little IKEA dresser by type—pants at the bottom, shirts at the top, dresses in the middle, socks and undies in fabric-lined boxes from the Container Store. I sort her board books by color, putting the white and yellow-spined books on one cubed shelf, the blues and greens on another, and so on. Her book collection looks like a rainbow. I buy her big bottles of finger paint in blue, red, yellow, and white—so that I can teach her color theory and how primary colors blend to create new ones. I want her life to be beautiful, from the outside in. Not because I'm superficial, but because I believe that a clean, organized environment will create a clean, organized life. In Japan—an island nation with a dense population—space is at a premium and people often live in smaller homes, especially in the cities. Efficient organizing and having fewer belongings is more than a national preoccupation; it's a survival skill. We love squirreling things away in little drawers. We have bespoke containers for everything—pencil cases, bento boxes, and tiny compartments for trinkets. Restaurants often provide crates that you can put your own bag in, so that it doesn't end up hanging off the side of a chair or sitting on a dirty floor.

When everything has a place, you're less likely to have clutter—at least, not the chaotic, disorganized kind. Ideally, everything that is visible *and* not visible should be clean and organized. When I ask my Japanese friends what surprises them most about the difference between American and Japanese culture, most of the answers are related to cleanliness.

"I once visited an American friend at their home. The living room and dining room were beautifully decorated and there was not a toy in sight," a Japanese friend tells me. "But inside the closet, there was a giant stack of unfolded clothes and bunched-up blankets—and toys strewn all over the floor!"

"Americans have a fundamentally different understanding of the concept of a floor," one friend marvels. "They'll put their feet up on a table, or sit down on the pavement, or walk into a house with shoes on."

A mom who transferred her kids from Japanese public school to American public school was shocked to see that kids didn't tidy up after themselves in a classroom. "They know that a janitor is going to clean up the classroom after they leave, so they don't even bother. And the teachers don't encourage it either, so they never learn."

Until I literally gave birth and brought my baby back to my house, I had no idea how Japanese my mothering tendencies would be. Before kids, I didn't think about whether all my furniture was matchy-matchy or if there were dust bunnies in the corner of the living room that nobody ever sees. But now that I live with children, I find myself trying to hold our family to Japanese standards of organization, cleanliness, and anal-retentiveness. Part of it is that kids are dirty and messy and chaotic. Keeping things in the same color scheme and mopping the floors every few days gives me back a sense of control in an otherwise unpredictable new reality. But also, it just feels necessary, like it's part of my role as a mom to make sure things are the way they are supposed to be. Is maternal instinct a myth? Misogyny? There's a big debate about this—and honestly, I don't know where I stand on it. All I know is that the little almost-subconscious actions I've suddenly adopted feel very Japanese mom–like. I obsess over the perfect containers for everything from Tupperware to kids' colored pencils to pantry items. I organize towels by use—hand towels, kitchen towels, and rags. It becomes harder and harder for Hubby to keep up with my new rules of the household. His idea of organizing is to put everything in ziplock bags. When I take photos of mismatched towels drooping unevenly off the sink and send them to him with funny-faced emojis to try to lighten the message, he sends me a ha-ha comment back, but the behavior does not change.

One day, N and I organize our shoe rack so that Hubby's shoes are in the bottom row, mine are in the middle, and hers are in the top row. In order of size. Makes sense, right? When N gets home from school, she kicks off her shoes, and on a good day, she'll put them on the top rack, facing forward, right shoe next to left shoe. Hubby puts his wherever there is an opening. Every other day, I'm standing in front of the shoe rack playing shoe Tetris, reordering them so that his shoes are on the bottom rack, mine are in the middle, and N's are at the top. Finally, one day, I ask him if he noticed that there is an organizing method to the shoe rack. He looks at me with a blank stare. "I just put the shoes where there is an opening," he says. "I thought that was what a shoe rack was for." He is not wrong. But my Japanese mom shoe rack is organized by whose shoes they are—in the same way that our books are organized by color and clothes are organized by function.

I also try really, really hard to make sure our family is on time to group outings. When it comes to our relationship with punctuality, Hubby and I could not be more different. When we first met, he used to travel a lot, hopping on a plane every other week to some beautiful destination in Europe or Africa. I am the type of flyer who knows exactly how long my flight is and has a loose agenda of what I'm going to do based on the duration of the trip. Hubby, on the other hand, never knows how long his flights are—nor does he feel the need to know. "What's the point?" He says, "I get on the plane at the exact same time as the person next to me. And we get there at the exact same time." He carries this lax attitude with him wherever he goes, which drives me nuts when I'm trying to show up as the punctual family. "It's not your job to get your Hubby places on time," someone tells me. But it feels like it *is* my job, along with many other invisible jobs that I—and no doubt other moms (not just in Japan but all over the world)—inevitably carry.

Sometimes even I get tired of my own expectations of cleanliness and organization of the household, but I can't stop. I find myself neurotically moving things from one side of the house to the other, frowning and tsk-tsking at little flecks of bread that invariably drop in front of Hubby's plate, the cream cheese smudges on the carpet under N's booster chair. I literally can't get that voice out of my head that says there is a way that it *should* be. On weekends, while my husband and daughters sprawl out on the living room floor surrounded by a dozen little mismatched toy trinkets and magazines folded in half and chipped tea mugs, I find myself rushing around them like a maniac, shuttling children's books and tiny folded toddler pants back and forth from various corners of the house to their designated spots (spots that only I am aware of the designation of), muttering to myself about how messy it is, my phone in one hand as I try to find cheap storage solutions that will help create a little more of a sense of order in this chaotic life.

In Japanese this is called osekkachi. It's the art of shuffling around to do little tasks and is commonly used to describe Japanese moms. It's not just me who suffers from this obsession. Some of my Japanese mom friends sanitize their kids' chairs every day. They vacuum all the floors at least every other day using fancy vacuum cleaners that give them dust scores, and buy washable rugs so they can throw them in the laundry. They cook fresh meals for their husband and children daily (one friend has a Notes doc where she maps out the menus for the week every Sunday night). They bathe their kids every day (I don't do this, but it is customary in a Japanese household). Some of my Japanese mom friends have never used a babysitter or hired a house cleaner because it still doesn't feel quite right to them to delegate these types of tasks, tasks that should be done by the mom. How does the saying go? You can take the Japanese mom out of Japan, but you can't take Japan out of the Japanese mom.

At CB, a school run by Japanese moms, books are organized by size, shape, and theme. Toys are put away in neutral-colored boxes and containers by category. For a room that is occupied by a bunch of toddlers all day, it has a pleasant amount of negative space—there aren't too many things in it. Sensei has a back office where she keeps extra books and places a curated selection on a simple wooden shelf that lines the classroom's eastern wall. The classroom itself is cheerful but neat: neutral colors, soft shapes, no plastic bags sticking out from the sides of things. Sensei always displays the children's most recent artwork on the wall, each perfectly spaced out on the north wall next to the clock: a dragon made of clay to symbolize the beginning of the Year of the Dragon, colorful foam Easter eggs in the spring, the full moon with some mochi cakes pasted onto a night sky for the summer solstice, papier-mâché autumn leaves in the fall.

Sensei and her team vacuum the school classroom every day, and it shows—there are no smells, no dust bunnies. Kids' dirty things are returned home neatly tucked into reused plastic bags. CB is for two-to-five-year-olds, so the students aren't mopping floors or running vacuum cleaners, but the teachers do, every day, and watching them do so has inspired N to think that sweeping and mopping are fun activities to do at home. The kids get stickers for tidying up after themselves or for helping others put toys away in the right containers. "When children participate in cleaning, they learn responsibility, mindfulness, and respect for their surroundings," Sensei says. "A well-organized space also minimizes distractions and helps children focus, fostering a sense of calm and order that enhances learning." I wholeheartedly agree with her. She's preaching to the choir! This is how I know she's in the right place, I tell myself.

But my biggest organizational inspiration comes from the other moms in the CB community. During an extended school break, Hubby and I take the girls on an overnight trip to the Pacific Coast together with another CB family. We stay at a little roadside hotel and buy tickets to an outing at the Monterey Bay Aquarium. It's cold and rainy, and we are each dealing with different moments of chaos and meltdown throughout the trip. The other mom, Satomi, is always full of joyful energy and impeccably prepared for any situation. I learn a lot by watching how she navigates the world with two rambunctious toddler girls in tow. She is a little bit like Doraemon—the famous anime robot cat invented by award-winning manga team Fujiko Fujio—whose magic pocket contains gadgets and tricks to solve every imaginable problem. On the first night of our trip, the kids order some orange juice, but it comes with a stick-straight paper straw that is too long for them to maneuver, and quickly gets shriveled up from too much chewing. Satomi reaches into her husband Greg's boxy gray backpack and pulls out multicolored reusable silicone straws. When N has to pee at a seafood restaurant but refuses to sit on the scary toilet seat, Satomi pulls out an oversized disposable toilet seat cover with unicorns and rainbows on it. "Use this!" she says. "I always carry one around." Before we turn in for the night, I peek into their hotel room and see that she's set up a portable crib next to an inflatable toddler bed. Even though we've returned only a few minutes ago, her two kids are in the bath and she's scrubbing them clean. Satomi is organized and efficient in a way that I can only aspire to be. N and M still have their shoes on and are wandering the hallways of the hotel. I need to learn her secret.

The next day, while we're walking around the waterfront with the four kids, M sneezes and a huge glob of snot comes out of her nose. Satomi reaches for Greg's backpack and voilà! A packet of wipes appears from the most easily accessible side pocket. "Can I please look at how you organize your mom bag?" I ask her, finally. "How do you always pull out the exact thing we need in a matter of seconds?" I peek into the big boxy backpack and see four small, simple gray pouches, placed in perfect Tetris formation inside the main compartment of the bag. It literally takes my breath away—there is not a stray bunny cracker or diaper to be seen. Inside each pouch, she explains, is a category of things. "This one is for snacks. This one is for other food-related items, like straws and spoons and bibs. This one is for toiletries—wipes, diapers, toilet covers like the one N used at the restaurant. This one is for extra clothes. You always need extra clothes," she adds, looking pointedly at M, who is pouring a cup of water down her shirt and pants. A pack of wipes is placed in a handy side pocket because they are the most frequently accessed item in the bag. The front pocket has water bottles, one for each kid.

I look sadly at my giant tote bag, which is filled to the brim with stuff. It looks like I'm carrying around a random sampling of things that are usually scattered all over my house and my life. When I reach into my bag, I never know what I'm going to get. Stray lip gloss. Spilled popcorn. A giant wad of napkins that I stuffed in there once, in case I might need them to wipe up a spill. Capless markers that have turned the entire interior of my tote a mess of pink and purple lines (lest I forget—they are N's favorite colors). But alas, no extra clothes for M, who is now soaked to the skin with ice water from her cup. Every outing is preceded by a chaotic hustle of preparing kids and things, and we still manage to forget something every time. The irony of having too much stuff, I realize, is that I can never find what I need when I need it. The signal-to-noise ratio is simply not in my favor. The beauty of having only the essentials organized in a systematic way is that I would always find what I need, and only what I need. This is the valuable lesson I take away from studying Satomi's mom bag.

The week after we get back from our Pacific Coast trip, I get to work putting together my best, most organized mom bag. There's no need to buy everything from scratch, I decide; I already have too much stuff. We have a big red Nike backpack, so I decide to repurpose this as our communal parent bag. I like the way Satomi has set up the roles and responsibilities in her partnership; she's the organizer and her hubby is the mule who carries it around. I rummage through the bathroom to find four modest-sized pouches to hold the different categories of items. It takes a little bit of trial and error to get it right, but in a few short months I too have become an expert Japanese mom bag packer. (Skip to p. 187 for a quick tutorial on how to make your very own Japanese mom bag!)

Life with kids can be incessantly chaotic. But maybe it doesn't have to be . . . right? If we can train ourselves to be less random and more organized, and then encourage our kids to follow suit, then we as a family become stewards of a more peaceful environment—at home, in our communities, and outside in the world.

Kenya Hara, Japanese lifestyle brand MUJI's famous art director, once said, "Design is not about decoration. It's a fundamental act of structuring the world, a shared language that allows people to connect and understand." If you walk into a MUJI flagship store, you'll know instantly what he means. There's always super-chill instrumental music in the background. The lighting is soft. Rows and rows of product are organized by category, then size, then color. And there are only natural colors because almost everything this brand makes is either cream, white, gray, or a natural wood tone. This is the type of precision and commitment that I aspire to uphold for the space that my family lives and breathes in. What's so crazy about that?

This is similar to the idea upon which Marie Kondo built her tidying-up empire. In her bestselling book *The Life-Changing Magic of Tidying Up*, Kondo took a concept that is fundamental to Japanese culture—that respect for our belongings and our surroundings is an essential step toward a harmonious environment—and transformed it into a global phenomenon. Kondo wasn't always the queen of clean. She was simply a person who loved organizing things. When she was in college, she started a small consulting business. Eventually, she turned her obsession into a brand, and today she has sold more than 14 million books, launched two Netflix series, and trained more than 850 certified consultants in fifty-four countries featuring the KonMari Method, her sweet yet strict and unabashedly Japanese-feeling version of *Home Makeover*. "The objective of cleaning is not just to clean, but to feel happiness living within that environment," she says in her saccharine, humble but somehow authoritative voice. Marie Kondo's basic folding method video has almost 14 million views on YouTube. Wearing a perfectly crisp cream-colored shirt, she folds a T-shirt, a camisole, and a pair of socks so neatly and lovingly that they stand on their side. "Oh look, it stands up!" she says with delight. When you can fold an unwieldy shirt so perfectly that it can stand on its side, then you can organize just about everything!

Kondo doesn't just organize your stuff. She teaches people to honor and appreciate their things—even the ones you're throwing away. "If you are letting go of an item, giving thanks is also a way of properly saying goodbye, so that you can mark the end of your relationship with the item and release it without guilt," she says. The world loves the KonMari Method because it helps us humanize things that we've numbed ourselves to in the Western world, like that fleeting feeling of grief that we feel when we part with a favorite pair of pants or whittle down our collection of crap that is no longer serving us. She gives us a way to process our more subtle and less tangible feelings of loss and separation and moving on. By celebrating the passing on of even the most ordinary things, we process our grief, no matter how trivial or irrational it might feel at first.

Many Japanese people have been practicing Marie Kondo–style super-obsessive organizing since we were kids. It's part of the training we've been indoctrinated with since we were little. The Japanese are animists. We believe that everything has a spirit. Even mundane daily items that are no longer in use get a grand farewell. Shrines offer final resting places not just for humans who have passed but for knives and other discarded items. At the end of the year, people bring their things to a giant bonfire where they are burned and their spirits are put to rest. In Zen Buddhism, cleaning and organizing our surroundings are vehicles for cultivating the mind. Daily housework is an opportunity to practice mindfulness. Japanese Buddhist monk Shoukei Matsumoto writes in his book *A Monk's Guide to a Clean House and Mind*, "We sweep dust to remove our worldly desires. We scrub dirt to free ourselves of attachments. . . . Everyone in today's busy world needs to do it. Life is a daily training ground, and we are each composed of the very actions we take in life. . . . If your heart is pure, the world looks brighter. If your world is bright, you can be kinder to others."

Japan is not a religious country, but our cultural landscape is filled with influences from both Shinto and Buddhist traditions. From a natural environment perspective, Japan is extremely eco-diverse, from the cloudlike snow that blankets the Hokkaido mountains to the lush forests of Yakushima to the tropical beaches of Okinawa. Forest bathing grew out of a Zen mindfulness practice and represents our deep respect for all living things and the healing and purifying power of the natural world. The Japanese believe that being in tune with nature is essential to our health and well-being, both personal and communal. In Shinto, Japan's indigenous belief system, nature is considered divine, and mountains, rivers, and trees house various deities commonly referred to as kami. We celebrate the changing of the seasons with the same reverence and enthusiasm as any major holiday. Our national holidays are called The Day of the Ocean, The Day of Respecting the Elders, and The Day of Respecting the Emperor. It's not considered religious to go to a shrine on New Year's or to honor your ancestors during Obon season. Every good Japanese person goes to a Shinto shrine in the first few days of the year to pray for good luck and get blessings, but it's less a religious rite and more of a cultural practice. When I was seven and my brother five, we put on kimonos for Children's Day to celebrate the fact that we had made it to these milestone ages (a tradition that still stands from when infant mortality was more prevalent). At age twenty, I put on a kimono once again and my parents hired a photographer who took pictures of me sipping holy water and ringing the bell at Meiji Shrine to signal my adulthood. Many restaurants, homes, and even offices have altars for their ancestors and the Shinto gods, where we place little bowls of rice and other condiments from our meals—a symbolic gesture to show that even after death, we take care of one another.

Even though they're thousands of miles away from the epicenter, the CB community also follows the drumbeat of seasonal festivities from the motherland. In January, for the New Year, they have a mochi-pounding festival and each kid takes turns hurling an oversized wooden pestle around in an attempt to turn plain cooked white rice into the popular glutinous rice cake. With the help of a few dads who hand-churn the giant mound of steaming grain as the kids pound it, the group eventually achieves the desired goal. They then hand off the Play-Doh-like blob to a crew of moms, who tear it into dozens of doughnut hole–sized chunks of mochi, which are seasoned in chestnut sauce, red bean paste, and classic soy sauce with nori seaweed, and distributed one at a time by the teachers. In February, there is Setsubun, and as the kids do back home, N throws soybeans on the schoolyard while repeating a chant that brings fortune inside and keeps bad luck outside. She comes home with three soybeans in a tiny cup, one for each year that she's been on this planet. In March, on Girls Day, N comes home with cardboard cutout ohinasama dolls while humming songs about springtime and the Girls Day festival. In May, for Children's Day, she makes paper carp flyers tied together with string that we put up in her bedroom window. Through art projects and seasonal songs, kids connect with Japanese culture in a natural and visceral way.

There is science-backed evidence that kids who grow up with routines and rituals have better outcomes across many different parts of their lives. They're physically healthier. They tend to develop a stronger sense of identity and do better in school. Some researchers have tracked children well into adulthood and found that those who had set routines and rituals in their early lives had better marriages and were generally happier. The American Psychological Association defines routine as something that happens on a reliable schedule and builds habits, like buying milk from the store at the beginning and end of each week or going to a music lesson every Friday. Rituals are more powerful and intrinsic. They bring people together and create a sense of belonging, sometimes even across borders or generations. Almost every parenting expert, no matter what their philosophy, says that consistency is how kids learn to self-regulate and get organized. "Routines are healthy and have many benefits for children," says Dr. Siggie Cohen, my favorite Instagram therapist, who happens to live near me and agrees to have a chat. "Repetition is how they learn. When things repeat themselves, it gives them a sense of confidence, and their accumulated experience allows them to rely on knowing what is expected and what they should then do next."

N begins and ends her meals with hands in prayer, saying itadakimasu! (bon appetit!) and gochisousama! (I have finished). On weekends, she likes to pretend she is the teacher at her day care. She does this wherever she finds books—in her bedroom, in our family living room, in the kids' section of a bookstore. She sits with her back straight, head held high, a collection of books as large as she can carry next to her chair. Then she announces, "Story time hajimaru yo hajimaru yo!" (Story time is beginning!) This is my cue to stop whatever I'm doing and pay attention to her. Once she has my full attention, she bows, her eyes closed, her hands on her knees, and says, "Yoroshiku onegai shimasu." (Thank you for being here. I look forward to working with you.) Then with a dramatic pause she picks up the first book and starts pretend-reading. She reads one book after another, *The Very Hungry Caterpillar* in English, *Nontan* in Japanese. Sometimes at home she puts on her sparkly blue heels, hoists a pink shoulder bag with colored pencils in it, picks up her favorite unicorn toy, tucks a board book under her arm, and says, "Otsukaresama deshita!" (You must be so tired from having worked a long and hard day!) And she walks out of the living room and into her room. A few minutes later she comes stomping out in her heels with a pile of pink fabrics—a do-rag, an apron, a kimono top—and plops everything and herself on the couch. "Ohayo!" (Morning!) she says. "Ohayo gozaimasu!" (Good morning!)

"Ohayo gozaimasu!" I say back. Then, she proceeds to do the first few moves of Bon Odori, a traditional summer festival dance performed in honor of our ancestral spirits.

Having a shared sense of purpose and a collective identity can be reassuring and lovely. But we also need to make sure they don't restrict kids from exercising their own free will. "Structure and a sense of safety are important," Dr. Siggie tells me. "But so is balance. We also want to make sure things aren't too rigid and inflexible. Life is such that once in a while, we should be off our path and see that we can cope and manage and always come back to what it is before. Being rigid is actually more fragile than being flexible."

N, for one, seems to be toggling between her collective identity as a Japanese-ish kid and her American-bred freedom in her own way. She seems to feel different emotions when she's speaking Japanese versus when she's speaking English. N-chan, the Japanese-speaking version of N, is sweeter, better behaved. She moves differently from her American counterpart; she sings rhythmically with a type of restraint that I see in the kids singing on Japanese TV, and her intonations are melodious and singsong—likely something she picked up from her friendly Japanese-speaking teachers at school. N-chan is more considerate and caring of others and says sweet things in Japanese like "Daijobu yo!" (It's okay!) and "Shimpai shinai de ne!" (Don't worry!) when she sees other people experiencing challenging emotions. N-chan has mastered the art of kizukai, an ability to care about others from the heart, the fingertips, the soul—but not in a showy way. It's close to empathy, but it's a lot more than just that. It's about a constant concern with the well-being of those around you. She also does not give hugs or kisses—her love, like Japanese love, is more reserved, more observant, less me me me and more communal. When I read her stories in Japanese, she sits straighter and listens more intently. The American version of N is more of a threenager, with occasional toddler tantrums and "I don't want to!"s. She subconsciously switches back and forth between the two languages based on what kind of mode she wants to be in. If she's resisting something, it's almost always in English. If she wants to be sweeter and more childlike, she switches to Japanese. Adults look wide-eyed at N-chan's stellar behavior, this tiny little curly-haired brown kid who speaks in full adult sentences in two languages, orders her own drinks at coffee shops, and sits quietly in the parents' chair at the doctor's office when accompanying me.

The same request made in Japanese yields a much more agreeable response than if I ask in English. Part of this, I realize, is a semantic issue: In Japanese, requests sound more like gentle statements than questions or commands. "Ofuro haitte ne" and "Ofuro hairu jikan desu yo" sound much more fun and convincing than "Can you take a bath?" or "It's time to take a bath"—even though they mean the exact same thing. I use Japanese as a tool to get her into a calmer and more obedient mode. It's a useful hack that I try not to exploit but appreciate having in my toolbox. I still resort to other tricks of parenting, like bribery with sugar, ominous countdowns, the promise of a surprise adventure. Of course, N and N-chan both have classic toddler challenges like not being able to seamlessly transition from one task to another or refusing help with things she believes, often mistakenly, she can do herself.

I take cues from the tools I've seen in Japan and try to build my own little mini society within our home. I call out a singsong "Okaerinasai!" (Welcome home!) whenever N enters the house, no matter what mood she is in, to set the tone for our time at home. We set alarms to signal when it's time to transition. We play the clean-up song at the end of the day and try our very best to get her to pick toys up off the floor. I print out worksheets from MEXT (the Ministry of Education, Culture, Sports, and Technology) and try to get N to think through some ethical challenges. Whenever she says things like, "I can do whatever

I want!" I counter it with phrases like, "Sometimes, but only if it doesn't cause other people trouble," and "When you finish doing all your responsibilities, then you can have some playtime."

In times of triage parenting, speaking to N-chan is also my secret weapon. I can get through to her better by communicating with the calmer part of her psyche in the language it best understands: Japanese!

FIVE

A Day in the Life of a Japanese Hoikuen

One summer, when N is almost four and M is almost one, we spend two months in Tokyo as a family. We cram into the very back row of United Airlines economy class, Hubby and me surrounding N, who is in the middle seat, while passing baby M back and forth between us. We even have our sixteen-year-old dog Malcolm with us. He's tucked under the seat in front of me, a seasoned traveler who knows to hibernate in his carrier until we arrive at our destination. N watches Disney movies while munching on snacks handed out by a friendly flight attendant, and Hubby walks up and down the aisle with M to keep her entertained. When we finally arrive eleven hours later, we're tired but excited about the adventures ahead of us. A white-gloved taxi driver in a dark gray suit somehow manages to Tetris our three giant suitcases, a massive stroller bag, and a couple of other stray items into his boxy trunk, and off we go to my brother's apartment, where we will be living for the next six weeks.

My brother lives on a tiny one-way street in Tokyo. Even though the neighborhood itself is surrounded by skyscrapers and highways, his street feels like a serene sanctuary, an escape from the urban jungle that is literally just a couple hundred feet away. Within a few blocks there's a supermarket that sells vegetables from regional farms and fresh sashimi; three medical clinics—one for adults, one for kids, one for pets; and a handful of restaurants that are open late at night—a ramen shop, an izakaya (pub), and a convenience store. It's also pin-drop quiet at night, even though there are a fair number of people walking around. His place is large by Japanese standards, though most Americans would probably think of it as a compact apartment. He has a narrow open-concept kitchen typical of many newer Japanese homes, and a Japanese-style bathroom, where the toilet is in a separate room from the bath and shower, and the bath area is separated from the changing area, usually by a frosted glass door. (While we have been bathing like this for centuries, the rest of the world is just catching on to this idea of having a "wet room," with major design and architecture publications calling it "the next big bathroom renovation trend.")

The four of us and Malcolm occupy a single room and sleep on three futons that we spread out on the floor. Historically, futons were laid down for sleeping time only, and the rest of the time they would be put away into closets so that the family could use the room as a living space. Families sleep in the shape of the character for river, 川, with a parent on each side and the child in the middle. This is what we do, sort of: We roll the futons up during the day so that we can use the floor space to play on, and at night, we spread them back out and all sleep together, in one room, on one floor. I place the futons perfectly straight next to one another with no gaps so that any snugglers can roll over seamlessly, but it's hot, and nobody wants to sleep under blankets lying straight. Every night, we take on a slightly different formation: Hubby on the far corner with M tucked under his arm while N spreads her arms and legs out on the far end and I wiggle my way in between the two girls; N asleep at the foot of the bed next to Malcolm's little bed, M in prime breastfeeding position; N going completely off script with her whole body stick straight on the wood floor because it's too hot for blankets. Sometimes, the girls fall asleep right next to each other. I'm not going to lie—I love it. It absolutely warms my heart to be this physically close to my kids, to be on the floor without having to worry about someone falling off the bed, to be able to roll from left to right and smell my kiddos. I love hearing N's soft and steady breath, I love singing to her when she's having a nightmare, the little requests that keep us up at night. *I need water, I need a foot massage, my bonnet fell off.* Living in America, I feel like I'm supposed to want to sleep next to my hubby and not my kids. My Western friends try to maintain the sanctity of their bedroom as a place for adult partners to unwind after kids hit the sack, but most of my Japanese mom friends still sleep with their kids. In Japan, on average, kids sleep with their parents until age ten. I think I understand why. It feels natural and healthy to be physically close to my kids when we're resting and restoring, like we're not fully separate humans yet.

It doesn't take long for us to find our rhythm in Tokyo. We spend a couple of days acclimating to our new surroundings, taking lots of walks, and hitting up some kid-friendly hot spots. We stock up on high-quality colored pencils, cute hair trinkets, and traditional toys at the hundred-yen store. We brave the weekend crowds to visit Rapunzel and Elsa at the new Fantasy Springs section of Disney Sea. We hang out at a fancy Starbucks that has a serene kids' space tucked into a corner of the kids' books section. A shoe rack at the entrance of the play area subtly signals to children that they should remove their shoes, and chill bossa nova music is playing at a low but audible volume on the sound system. N squeals in delight as she recognizes books featuring her favorite characters, Hello Kitty and Nontan and Pan Dorobo, an adventurous mouse disguised as a piece of white bread. When the afternoon heat gets unbearable, we pop into the nearest convenience store, which is filled with kids shopping for an after-school snack, college students and freelancers buying premade bento dinners, salarymen stocking up on energy drinks before going back to wrap up their work. Every day, at 5:00 p.m. sharp, a melodic song plays on the public loudspeakers across the country, signaling for everyone to go home. And everyone, for the most part, goes home.

We take a pilgrimage to the Anpanman Children's Museum in Yokohama. Self-sacrifice is a value that has dominated the Japanese psyche since the Shōgun days, and one of the most popular icons representing this value is Anpanman, a superhero whose face is made from freshly baked red bean bread. The anime series was conceived by the late genius animator Takashi Yanase, who served in World War II and faced starvation numerous times. His own life experience inspired the invention of a superhero who is made of food. With his round head, rosy cheeks, and pure personality, Anpanman flies around the world sacrificing his own face to save the world. "I am going to go patrol the world to make sure there are no hungry creatures out there!" Anpanman declares in the opening credits of the show before flying off into the night sky, arms outstretched like Superman. He shoots out of the bread factory chimney and over a windmill and scoops up a little yellow baby bird that has fallen out of a tree. He drops the baby bird back into its bed of twigs and then pulls a portion of his cheek off and sprinkles it on top of the nest, smiling and waving while the birds happily chirp and open and close their mouths as he flies away with a gaping hole on his head. Anpanman teaches selflessness and self-sacrifice in service of peace and harmony at all costs. He didn't become a globally renowned icon like his bright yellow peer Pikachu—his popularity has been largely focused on Japan and parts of Asia—but he is responsible for a massive empire of movies, TV shows, and endorsements worth sixty billion dollars. Japanese pharmacies sell Anpanman bandages, Anpanman eye drops, Anpanman mosquito patches. Japanese supermarkets sell Anpanman gummies, Anpanman yogurt, and, of course, Anpanman bread.

At the museum, we watch a strange stage show in which humans wearing full-body costumes of the main characters—a bacteria-like villain, a piece of white toast, a curry pastry, and of course, Anpanman—dance to disco music. Then, N spends a bunch of time in Dokin-chan's kitchen—a little semi-enclosed play area with signage stating that it belongs to the villain's needy, selfish, incredibly cute orange sidekick. Half a dozen kids under the age of four are busy playing in the kitchen, moving miniature pots and pans around, chopping plush vegetables with a plastic silver knife, turning the fake oven knob on and off. I notice that they are playing with a systematic rhythm, like they know exactly how they're supposed to play in a play kitchen. One kid is setting the table. Another is placing pancakes on plates. N, the ultimate observer, starts putting vegetables next to each pancake on the plates. Outside the room, five Japanese moms are watching quietly and not saying a word, just standing by and waiting for their kids to finish playing.

The museum is packed, and it feels busy, but it's not because the kids are running around or being chaotic. There are just a lot of people. Despite the density of people, the kids here are in flow—and the design of the space helps facilitate that flow. The museum has color-coded bathrooms—red for women, orange for wheelchair accessible, green for kids, blue for men, pink for the nursing room. The green area is equipped with kid-sized toilets and sinks low enough for kids to be able to use them without the help of an adult. I go to the nursing room with M, which has soothing pink walls and plays a classical music rendition of the Anpanman theme song accentuated by the sounds of babies suckling in the next-door stalls. When I'm done, I step out into the crowded cafeteria and admire the tables full of Japanese children sitting next to their parents, eating their themed curry rice and sandwiches happily and quietly. Anpanman isn't just here to entertain these kids. He is teaching them values like selflessness and community harmony.

One of my favorite memories of growing up as a kid in Japan was going to the bookstore and finding the latest furoku—bonus gifts strapped into the midsection of a magazine with a bellyband. Each furoku provides age-appropriate experiences that caregivers and children can share together. "We are in the business of selling experiences," explains Chiyo Takahashi, editor of the furoku magazine *BabyBook*, which targets kids ages zero to two. "Our furoku allow the tiniest children to role-play things that they might observe in the adult world, like shopping in a supermarket or riding a bus." A recent issue of *BabyBook* includes a battery-operated button that is an exact replica of the one you press when you want the bus to stop. "In actual life, if a kid pushes the button over and over on a real bus, they'll get in trouble. But if they do it with the toy, it's okay. And you can teach kids valuable lessons like 'Don't touch things in the supermarket!' or 'You can do it with the toy but not in real life.'" By using stickers and foldouts and pretend-play, these books create opportunities for parents and children to satiate their urge to do adultlike things while learning valuable societal lessons.

I buy N the latest issue of *Mebae*, the furoku magazine for three-to-five-year-olds. We build a three-dimensional amusement park on a two-page spread, complete with a cardboard tube roller coaster with elevated tracks and a cutout ride car that moves up and down the track; a parachute ride that slides up and down; and spinning teacups, each with little slits into which you can place a cutout version of manga characters. We prepare a Hello Kitty picnic spread from cut and folded paper, including onigiri, hamburger steak, a slice of orange, a baby-octopus-shaped sausage, an egg roll, a sandwich with veggies, broccoli, and a tomato. Each furoku requires fine-motor skills and a healthy dose of imagination for pretend-play. N and M get just as much joy from a paper amusement park or picnic as they do from the real thing—sometimes even more, especially when it's sweltering hot, and riding imaginary roller coasters with their favorite anime characters is way more fun and interactive than sitting on the couch doing nothing.

One day, I sign up M for a course whose description loosely translates as "The Unlimited Possibilities of Children Baby Class." On the second floor of a pristine walk-up apartment building in the heart of a tiny shopping street in central Tokyo, a young woman with chin-length hair, a chirpy voice, and a happy smile rattles off flash cards like they're tongue twisters, counts off numbers on giant colorful abacuses, sings nature songs, hands the babies random toys to play with—all at breakneck speed. The entire class is exactly fifty minutes long, but it feels more like fifty hours. By the end I am exhausted, and so is M, but the other moms seem to be enjoying themselves. What's the secret? "Adults and babies have a very different sense of time," explains the instructor. A brochure from this school says that the average IQ of kids coming out of their school is 140. (This is a higher average, they say, than Tokyo University entrants, who have an average IQ of 130.) "A good brain is the number one present Mom and Dad can give to their kids," the woman explains. "If you develop their language skills at this age, zero to eight months, then they won't have problems learning when they're in middle school and high school. If you don't, that synapse never develops. And it's not just language. Same with math! By flashing numbers quickly past their brain, very specifically timed at one number per second, they create math synapses in their brains. Did you see the babies' faces? They are so focused!" She sends me home with a marketing brochures that reminds me: It's never too early to start exercising my baby's brain!

The Japanese have come up with a genius solution for getting people to follow the rules of society, which is to make everything relentlessly cute. Cuteness is a national obsession, a business case, a political tool, a foundational value that can be found underneath the hood of almost every major effort this country undertakes. It's also a nationally sanctioned visual language, a part of our core brand identity. When you visit the country, you'll see kawaii things everywhere—hand-drawn mascots reminding people to stay out of construction sites, cute animal figurines urging passersby to enter an otherwise obscured storefront, tiny trinkets adorning the handbags of even the most stoic-looking adult commuter. When even super-serious things are cute, people can more easily build a connection with them and pay attention to the message they're trying to relay. This helps society inform and instruct evenly across all ages and interest groups.

In the late eighties and nineties, the Japanese government rolled out a series of cute mascot characters to become the brand representatives of their most serious law enforcement entities. I was in elementary school in Tokyo when a team of local police officers came to introduce Pipo-kun, a fuzzy orange rodent-fairy type of creature with Mickey Mouse ears, anime eyes, and a pointy blue and yellow antenna on his head that, according to his biography written on the official police force website, acts as a transponder for any unusual goings-on about town. "Meet Pipo-kun!" said the policeman and policewoman who accompanied a real life-sized Pipo mascot, "the newest addition to the Tokyo Metropolitan Police Department!"

In Japan, most cops don't carry guns or tasers or other scary weapons. In general, they are not very scary; sometimes it seems like their main job is riding around on their bicycles, managing traffic in increasingly busy urban streets, and administering their extensive lost-and-found system. Until then, interactions with the Japanese police were not part of my childhood psyche, but after meeting Pipo-kun, I felt a sort of positive connection to them that didn't exist before and became more aware of their role in society. Virtually every major public institution in Japan has a cute mascot character as part of their labor force—prefectural police departments, the Fire and Disaster Management Agency, the Japan Ground Self-Defense Force, even prisons. "Prisons have the image of being isolated places that have no contact with the rest of society and are surrounded by imposing grey walls," a PR officer at Asahikawa Prison told the Associated Press. "We made a mascot to change the image into that of a facility open to society and supported by society." Asahikawa Prison is represented by a life-sized square-faced mascot with a purple flower hat called Katakkuri-chan, named after dogtooth violet, a flower that blooms in the northern region where the prison sits.

A study published by a team of Oxford neuroscientists in 2016 showed that cuteness fires rapid neurons in the orbitofrontal cortex, which is linked to pleasure. There is nothing like a message delivered by a cute stuffie to get a kid to listen attentively and joyfully follow instructions. The Japanese people use cuteness to indoctrinate children into becoming upstanding citizens of our world. A cute cartoon character is better at reinforcing societal values and ideas than lectures and words. The rest of the world knows this, too, but Japan takes it to a whole new level. "In Japan, cuteness is not just an aesthetic; it is a cultural code, a form of communication, and a powerful tool of consumer capitalism. It simplifies and sweetens the complexities of life, making them more palatable and marketable," writes Japanese culture expert Sharon Kinsella in her essay "Cuties in Japan."

Every night, N brushes her teeth while attempting to rescue a captive Pokémon in a cute app by polishing away her little pearly whites while wearing a Pikachu cap. The app uses augmented reality to dress kids up in Pokémon hats and track how well kids are brushing away all the bacteria. If N does a good job, she gets to dust off and catch a new Pokémon, which gets added to her virtual Pokedex.

"Kuchu kuchu pe," she says after brushing her teeth, mimicking the sound of water swishing in her mouth and then spitting.

"Goshi goshi," she says as she scrubs her hand under the sink, carefully spreading the soapsuds between each of her tiny fingers.

These onomatopoeias are powerful tools, I realize. It's much more fun to tell a kid, "It's goshi goshi time!" than to plead with them to wash their hands. The Japanese language has more than 4,500 onomatopoeic words. Daily tasks like brushing teeth and using the toilet are always associated with cute-sounding onomatopoeias. "Things can feel very serious sometimes, especially to children," says a female scientist on Japanese TV, who claims to be an expert on onomatopoeia. "That's why we use sound effects to make it more accessible."

Here are a few other onomatopoeias that you're likely to see in a Japanese-inspired child's daily life:

Yoisho = the sound of picking up something heavy from the floor

Unnnn = the sound of a child trying to poop

Kuchu kuchu pe = the sound of a child rinsing their mouth

Jabu jabu = the sound of water coming out of the faucet

Chapu chapu = the sound of rain boots splish-splashing through a puddle

Goshi goshi = the sound of tiny hands being scrubbed together

Poi = the sound of throwing away garbage

Being in my hometown of Tokyo with an infant and a toddler, I experience omotenashi in a whole new way. Many department stores and other public venues have secluded spaces where parents can spend time with their kids without having to worry about disturbing other people. These family rooms start to feel like a necessity for any outing—and very thoughtfully designed. One shopping mall family room we visit sits behind a translucent automatic sliding door that opens into a spotless white space with great lighting and a city view. There's a small seating area with soft, easy-to-climb sofas and chairs that kids can't get hurt on; a row of changing tables with wipes and diaper disposal bins right nearby; a couple of private nursing stalls equipped with a chair, a table, and a coat hook—cordoned off by accordion doors for extra privacy. A small kitchenette equipped with a sink and a machine provides purified, sterilized, room temperature water that parents can use to make formula. Everything is clean and spotless. There is no hair on the ground, no toilet paper strewn all over the place, no unflushed toilets. There's a small bookshelf with a dozen books for different age groups and a vending machine selling juice and coffee, so that kids and parents can have a little R & R before going back out into the rest of the world. Just because this is a designated family room doesn't mean you can let your kids run wild in here. It is spotless, and frequented by cleaning staff who ensure there is no diaper stink in the air or crumbs left on the floor. And if your kids are causing too much noise or running in the space, a security guard is never too far away. On one visit, N put her foot on top of a low table designed for eating and playing, and a woman in a uniform appeared out of nowhere and asked her quietly to step down from the table.

One day, I forget something at a yakiniku place after having dinner with my friend Daisuke and two of his kids. It's a fun but rowdy dinner and we leave the pristine floor-seated room a complete mess. On our way out, we knock over a small folding screen painting, and there's rice and beef all over the otherwise spotless floor. In the chaos of getting the kids out in one piece, I leave M's sippy cup on the table. When I go pick it up the next day, a tall man in a suit greets me at the door of the restaurant. Before I even say a word, he puts his hand up in immediate recognition, rushes to the counter where the host is, and pulls out M's sippy cup, which has been deep cleaned and neatly wrapped in plastic. "Thank you so much for coming back," he says, bowing repeatedly. "I'm sorry we did not notice right away; we were too slow."

It's also much easier to get medical care here—even without health insurance. When N comes back from a park with massive wasp-bite welts, screaming in pain, her skinny little legs covered in swollen red blotches, we are able to get immediate care from a pharmacist at a nearby drugstore. The pharmacist, a young man in a white lab coat, asks N a few questions, in a calm and steady adult voice. "Where did you get these bites?" "Do they itch or just hurt?" After a quick assessment, he gives her a steroid cream and some round sticky antihistamine bandages with a smiling Anpanman on them. After that, she doesn't complain much about the bites anymore; instead, she talks incessantly about her Anpanman bandages and seems to have forgotten why she needed them to begin with.

In Japan, most people have social health insurance and pay less than two thousand yen (about thirteen dollars) a visit when they go to the doctor; even if you don't have health insurance for some reason, anyone can walk into a doctor's office and get immediate, top-quality care for a fraction of the price they would pay in America. You don't need to wait four months to get a proper doctor's appointment, as is the case with our primary care practice back home. Even Hubby, who speaks no Japanese, was able to get cough medicine from the neighborhood pharmacist, who used a real-time translation app on his tablet to analyze his symptoms and make recommendations. (In contrast, just a couple of months earlier in California, M scratched her ear with a long fingernail and was walking around with blood dripping down the side of her face. I shuttled my bleeding baby from CVS to Rite Aid to a local private urgent-care center, and nobody—not the pharmacist, the receptionist, nor any passerby—seemed to care. "Sorry, we don't see children," the urgent-care clinic receptionist said. Then she went back to chatting with the other receptionist, giving me annoyed sideway glances until I finally walked out the door with my child, still bleeding.)

Because we're in Tokyo for an extended period of time and I have to work, we enroll N in a public day care center. Tiny Friends just opened a couple of years ago in an unassuming three-story concrete building in an urban residential neighborhood. The only way you can tell it's a day care center is because of the row of identical mamacharis (mom bicycles) parked outside the facility between 8:55 a.m. and 9:05 a.m. Each mamachari is a muted color, either a dark navy or charcoal gray, with a giant basket in front and a toddler bicycle seat behind, all in perfect condition without any scratches or identifiers. Every morning the moms glide into the bike parking aisle on their mamacharis in their comfy casual linen and cotton dresses, not a hair out of place, and greet one another sweetly in a singsong "ohayo gozaimasu!" Clearly, there are some standards in place for how we should appear when we drop off our children. I find myself questioning my outfit choices and having a little FOMO for not getting the memo on the unwritten expectations for moms taking their toddlers to hoikuen in this ritzy Tokyo neighborhood. Should I be procuring a closet full of flowy linen dresses for drop-off and pickup? Why aren't these moms covered in sweat? When did they have time to comb their hair to such perfection that not a strand is out of place?

The school asks N to bring a sun hat, indoor shoes, two sets of clothes every day, and two towels for naptime. What N brings to school is just as important as what she doesn't bring to school. I am asked not to include a water bottle in her backpack because they cannot guarantee the safety of what's in it. Instead, they ask me to pack a small cup (I get a Pokémon mug for three hundred yen at a pharmacy on my way home from work), and they give her freshly made barley tea along with everyone else in her class during planned interval breaks in the day. N also tells me that I should no longer pack her mosquito repellent because they have some at school. Laminated signs printed and placed near the day care door announce to parents what they need to be ready for that week. "Monday is nail check day. Please make sure you trim your kids' nails this weekend." "Next week we start pool days. Please look at your checklist to make sure you do the necessary preparations."

Getting a kid ready for the pool is a meticulous multistep process. The teacher hands me three forms to read and fill out. A "what to bring" checklist, a daily calendar showing which class goes in the pool on which day of the week, and another form with super-tiny print that we are to bring every day showing her morning body temperature and whether we consent to her going in the pool that day, signed and stamped (Japan still uses hanko, or official signatory stamps) by the parent, the schoolteacher, and the headmaster. This last form is submitted to the ward, presumably to prevent any liability issues should a child have an incident at the pool. Which seems unlikely, since it's just an inflatable rectangle sitting on an enclosed balcony, the type you often find in suburban American backyards.

I diligently check off the items on the checklist, and N shows up on the first Monday morning of July with a swimsuit, goggles, a swim cap, and a towel. That afternoon, Hubby picks her up. He doesn't speak Japanese, but he says something to me about N not having the right equipment for swimming. The next day I get the full download from a young male teacher: "She needs to bring a waterproof bag to put her things in"—he points to a little crate on the floor by the classroom entrance, where all the other kids have brought an identical tote made of clear vinyl with their swimming gear in it—"and she also does not need goggles."

The school has a daily curriculum, which is pasted on the wall.

9:20–30	Clean up
9:30	Water break Morning meeting
9:45	Outdoor activities Wash hands, clean up
11:45	Lunch Change clothes
12:45	Nap
15:00	Snack
16:00	Going home ceremony

Every afternoon before pickup, the teachers write an update on a little whiteboard for the parents to read about how the day's activities helped foster an important part of holistic learning—whether that was nurturing the body, learning the cultures and rituals of Japan, or expanding the children's awareness of the world. By giving us these updates, the teachers are informing us of the life lessons baked into their daily activities, so that we can talk to our kids about them and support them in their growth.

JULY 5 (FRIDAY)—SUNNY

ACTIVITY 1: LEARNING ABOUT THE TANABATA FESTIVAL

Goals: To learn about Tanabata (The Star Festival) and to become familiar with traditional festivals.

Today, the children took part in some Tanabata festivities. After quietly listening to the teachers read a book about the festival, the kids smilingly answered a pop quiz about what they had learned. Then, they created their own ornaments and presented them to the class.

ACTIVITY 2: PLAYING WITH THE PARACHUTE

Goals: To understand how the parachute works and how to control its movement. To develop an understanding of the jumping sensation in a safe environment.

We played with a para-balloon inside the classroom today. "What is this?" "How does it work?" They were full of curiosity. They threw it high up in the air, then made it small, and finally they danced with it to a children's song. Afterward during gym time, we practiced jumping over a rope.

The school bulletin board displays half a dozen photos describing the event of the day. One day, a dentist shows up at the school to do a complimentary dental check and teach kids how to take care of their teeth. On another, a semiprofessional soccer coach sets up drills on the third-floor play space and shows kids the fundamentals of footwork. One afternoon, three young women in floor-length princess dresses come and play classical music for the kids. N tells me all about it when she gets home. "The princesses, they came, and one was doing this tweet, tweet, tweet!"—she pretends to play a flute—"and two of them were playing the violin. And they played Disney songs!" This isn't just some musical band off the street; in the photos displayed on the bulletin board that afternoon, I see that these women are dressed as if they are performing at Carnegie Hall, not a day care center. By Japanese standards, it would be unthinkable to give a lesser-quality performance for kids than you would for adults.

N will go back to the United States after this summer, but the rest of her classmates are on track to stay in the Japanese school system—a robust, meticulous education machine designed to churn out humans who can maintain the beautifully organized social structures that this country relies on. "Our schools re-create an atmosphere that reflects the outside world. The students build and operate their own mini shakai (mini society)," Dr. Hiroshi Sugita, an education expert at Kokugakuin University in central Tokyo, tells me. If America emphasizes individuality first and then getting along with others, Japan is the exact opposite. "In the United States, you start with Who are you? What is unique about you? What are your strengths?" says Ema Ryan Yamazaki, a Tokyo-based mom and filmmaker who made an Oscar-nominated documentary about the Japanese school system. "In Japan, your identity is formed through how you contribute and how you fit in."

Japan has an impressive academic record—its students consistently score at the top of global exams, and the rate of students making it to high school is 98.7 percent, higher than any other modern country. But it's not just about that. They learn how to be a harmonious part of any group and prioritize cooperation over self-indulgence. School is where they learn how to be community members first. They take turns being the class leader, mopping floors, scrubbing blackboards, serving lunch, and sweeping the schoolyard. The class leader is in charge of making sure everything is getting done and in order—the equivalent of a manager at work. "For young children, there's a lot of benefit to being part of a collective, to learn how to care for others the same way you'd care for yourself," Ema says. "You're learning to be responsible—and to enjoy the weight of that responsibility."

In her 2023 film, *The Making of a Japanese*, Ema documents daily life at an elementary school in the Setagaya ward of Tokyo. One of the protagonists in the film is a first grader who has been chosen to play the triangle at a school performance of "Ode to Joy." This tiny girl has a little trouble getting the hang of things, and the teacher scolds her for not trying hard enough, bringing her to tears. It seems kind of harsh at first, but over time we start to understand that this is a lesson in resilience and hard work—not just an extracurricular for-fun activity. Just one instrument out of sync can ruin the whole orchestra . . . right?

We see her go through these intense emotional waves: pride at getting selected, shame at not having practiced enough, determination to do better, joy at being able to contribute to the bigger performance successfully with the other students. In many ways, the process of making this film reminded Ema of her own childhood. "My most vivid memories are sports days and music performances," she tells me. "Even back in my day, it was pretty normal to rehearse every day for an hour or two, four or five weeks leading up to the event." Activities like jumping rope and gymnastics are super-serious affairs, with lessons carefully designed to teach the complexities of teamwork through physical activity. Sarah Birke, the *Economist* reporter whose kids go to Japanese school in Mexico, once asked the principal of their school why they took jumping rope so seriously. It turns out there is a really good reason. "Skipping rope might seem like playground fun to us, but apparently it works on grand-motor skills and fine-motor skills, and the jump rope games are great for developing team-building and cooperation," she tells me.

The kids learn how to put values like kizukai and omotenashi into practice through lightly facilitated group conversations that encourage them to role-play difficult moments and see things from other people's perspectives. These practices have inspired world leaders from places as far away as Egypt and Malaysia. Egypt's president, Abdel Fattah el-Sisi, has adapted this practice into his nation's education system since 2014. And in Malaysia, the group discussion model is being used to better link the principles of Islamic religious education to daily activities with special emphasis on values like mutual caring and responsibility.

MEXT, Japan's education ministry, publishes downloadable manuals on how to instill moral education into every kid's life, from first grade on. Even the smallest grade-school kids are encouraged to ask themselves questions such as "What types of things do you need to pay attention to in order to follow the rules and have a pleasant day every day?" and "Look around you. There are many things you must do by yourself. What are you putting your efforts into?" Cute illustrations show a small child scrubbing a bathtub, sweeping the schoolyard, writing diligently in a notebook, pulling roots out from a flower bed. There's a list that kids can use to check off the days of the week and whether their textbooks and backpacks were stacked neatly. By doing this every day, they eventually learn to keep their things neat. "The atmosphere has incredible educational power," says Dr. Sugita.

After just a few weeks at her Japanese hoikuen, N is speaking crisper Japanese, and her vocabulary has expanded to include nuances and expressions that she would not have learned in the United States. Even more remarkably, her mannerisms have changed, and she has picked up some cool habits on how to keep her surroundings extra buttoned-up and tidy. She starts folding her undies into perfect little squares instead of stuffing them into a drawer. She cleans her toothbrush with a little towel after using it and wipes the sink down with a washcloth. She knows how to use just enough soap so that she doesn't waste any but still gets her hands sparkly clean. I appreciate this subtle lesson in portioning that she has received—in America, overindulgence and having too much is not necessarily considered bad, but here in Japan, they teach you exactly how much soap to pump so that you are not deviating from the norm or taking more than what belongs to you. N also starts eating differently after her first summer in Japan. She folds her hands together and says itadakimasu before digging in. She finishes almost everything on her plate. She asks politely for soup, which they regularly served with her lunches at Tiny Friends. When she is finished eating her meal, she folds her little rubber place mat perfectly around her little round plate before taking it to the kitchen. She asks us to check how well she brushed her teeth, no doubt a practice they do at her day care. She's much better at cleaning up her toys. And monitoring the length of her nails becomes a weekly routine at home.

Each of the activities she does in Japan makes her proud and furthers her confidence and independence in a way that I have not seen before. N is developing an overabundance of perceived autonomy—meaning, she thinks she is capable of way more than she actually is. It's as if her American-inspired free spirit and the Japanese-inspired self-sufficiency are mashed together in a strong-willed toddler, and all of a sudden she thinks she's a fully functioning adult. She seems to believe that she no longer needs my help to do most things, like use the toilet, buy snacks at a convenience store with my credit card, hold the door open for people getting on the elevator, and serve her own food from a buffet. "No, Mama, don't come with me," she says as her refrain, and "Thanks, but I already know."

She is fascinated by the autonomy she observes in other kids around her. She stares intently at the little boy around her age in a white collared shirt, navy-blue shorts, and a matching cap who has his own key to the building my mom lives in.

"Why is that kid by himself?" she asks me.

"He's on his way home."

"Are his mom and dad already at home waiting for him?"

"Probably! Do you think you can walk home by yourself?"

N thinks hard, then puts up three fingers and stares straight into my eyes. "No, because I'm only three! Tomorrow, when I'm four, maybe I can walk home by myself." After that day, though, whenever we approach the front door, she asks for the key so that she can unlock it herself. And she always holds the elevator door open for everyone, running in and diligently pressing the Open button until everybody and their appendages are safely inside.

American independence and Japanese independence have very different nuances. In Japan, early independence means being able to fulfill your role as a willing, participatory member of society. By the time they're in their late single digits, a Japanese child has learned how to get places on their own using public transportation, to buy what they need, to respectfully navigate the public sphere. Since the streets are pretty much devoid of unpredictable traffic and shady people, parents can send their little ones off on their own to do all kinds of things, like getting to lessons or visiting a friend's house. In America, independence means you have free will, that you have the right to speak up for what you want, what you don't want, and what you are therefore willing to do or not do. It also is tied to real logistical challenges, like the ability to drive. Because many parts of the United States are not walkable or not serviced by efficient public transportation, kids have to be driven everywhere until they can drive themselves—which means that what their parents do on the weekends is often determined by what the kids would also enjoy doing.

"In Tokyo, there was entertainment of all kinds at the tips of our fingers—literally we could walk to the aquarium or the movie theater," says Seiko, a mom of two who moved to Silicon Valley a couple of years ago. "In the United States, we are always in the car, the kids strapped in their car seats. We really try to make an effort to encourage them to enjoy being outside. We play pickleball and go to driving ranges to practice our golf swing, but it's so easy to default to just playing games and watching Netflix all day."

During our summer in Japan, N learns how to decorate a cake while wearing an adorable child-sized chef's jacket and exaggeratedly tall chef's hat. She learns about the cycle of grain cultivation by stomping through rice fields in galoshes and then eating fresh onigiri as a reward for her hard work. She bakes her own pizza in a real wood-fired oven. She buys bread with her own money at a bakery that only kids are allowed to shop in. The entryway is kid-sized, and inside there is allegedly a proper counter where kids can select a yummy pastry in exchange for 250 yen. The parents' only job is to make sure they have money and patiently wait outside—when I try to peek in to take a photo, I promptly get kicked out by a security guard dressed like a baker.

Everywhere I go, I see parents quietly observing their kids at play. Rather than getting involved, they stand at the perimeter and don't say a word. They just silently observe, like proctors at an SAT exam. Their job as parents is to give kids the tools and then trust that they'll use them. If you're micromanaging them while they're performing on the social stage, then you clearly didn't train them enough. In America, moms and dads are active participants in kids' playground games like tag and hide-and-seek, running after their children and climbing on the jungle gyms. Even if they're standing on the sidelines chatting with friends, they shout occasional commands or encouragements to their kids, maybe just to let them know that they're there. In Japan, for the most part, parents lightly supervise their children, intervening only if absolutely necessary.

Japanese society expects every kid and every adult to do their part in upholding the standards of society. No matter how Herculean an effort is required for everyone to adhere to these standards, especially with little rascals nipping at your feet, people do it. If you didn't, you would stand out like crazy and get dirty looks from everyone around you all the time. In California, N and her friends are the most well-behaved kids in town. But in Japan, they are clearly the worst. One weekend, a few of the CB families who are in Tokyo for the summer plan a group outing to the Fire Museum, a real six-story former working firehouse that has been transformed into a learning and play space. Here, kids can ride in a stationary helicopter and watch a simulation of putting out fires, wear firefighter suits and hold hoses and pretend to put out fake flames cast against a digital screen, and create their own augmented reality ambulance and watch it pick up people in emergency situations around a picture of a city. Even though it's sweltering hot and the AC in the place is barely keeping it breathable, the Japanese parents and their kids are waiting patiently in a single-file line for some of the more popular features, like the helicopter ride. Not our kids. N and her friends are hopping around, sticking their heads in the vehicle while other people are in it, giggling and squirming and definitely not standing quietly in a single-file line. I pretend not to notice the horror on the other parents' faces. What can we do? We are trying our best to wrangle them.

After the fire museum my friend Kana and I take our kids on a walk. It's drizzling, so we stop at a nearby café, buy some onigiri rice balls, and sit down on a bench in the least crowded section of the railroad-style diner. A lone woman in a plain white dress and a low ponytail reads an academic textbook while sitting quietly in the corner. Our kids start off fine; M munches on a sweet potato breadstick while N and Kana's kid share a rice ball. But it's midafternoon, and as any toddler parent knows, this is the time when kids start to get unruly. Sure enough, they start to whine and squeal for no apparent reason. This is when we get the first sideways glance from Academic Lady. At first, it's subtle. I can't tell if she's just gazing off from her book to think about something or actually expressing a very passive form of annoyance. Then, one of the kids kicks off their shoes. And her gazes away from the book become longer. She never actually looks directly at us, but her head tilts ominously in our direction, enough so that if I look at her (and I never do so directly, either—that would be rude!), it is now obvious to me that she is annoyed. Things only get worse. The kids start sliding around on the seat, slide off the seat, put their feet on the seat. By now they are breaking all the unwritten rules of how a child behaves in public and the woman's sideways glances have turned into a straight, head-on glare. Of course, we never apologize directly to her (that would be acknowledging her annoyance and facing the tension, which would be very un-Japanese of us). Instead we loudly admonish our children for misbehaving, pack up our stuff, and leave. Only after we have fully departed from our seats, our onigiri wrappers properly disposed of in the trash cans, our desecrated seats wiped down with baby wipes, does the woman's head go back to its original position, her eyes back on her book.

Kana and I shrug at each other. But truly, what can we do? It's witching hour!

One weekend, Hubby and I decide to take the kids on a short trip to a mountainside resort a couple of hours outside Tokyo. It's a serene and secluded retreat with a hot spring bath and forests worthy of bathing in on a honeymoon—and it also provides extremely kid-friendly amenities. Our hotel room comes with a complimentary child kit, which consists of a potty, a step stool, and a box full of Mega Bloks. The online restaurant reservation system presents us with an optional button to use if we want our kids to be taken care of, free of charge, at the adjacent play space—a giant domelike structure that has a lounge for adults on one side and a well-cushioned shoes-off area with a ball pit and a netted structure that looks like a cumulus cloud that kids can climb into and play in all day. The (free!) babysitting service includes a full-time caregiver for my two children and nutritious age-appropriate meals for both kids: beef curry and rice for N, and fish porridge for baby M. For breakfast, a hotel staffer helps us set up a picnic on the lawn, complete with a fully packaged meal of eggs, yogurt, pastries, coffee, cutlery, and little flower-shaped cushions to sit on.

At a highway rest stop on the way back, we find a special row of booth seats for families with small children. Everything is lower to the ground and painted a pastel green, and it's out of the way of other patrons who may prefer to have a quieter meal. Right next to the people-with-kids area is a nursing and changing room. The rest stop kiosk sells a very random but comprehensive selection of goods to satiate any fussy child, including princess jewelry and Pokémon cards. There are at least ten restaurants to choose from with a wide variety of food—beef tongue sandwiches, chicken-and-rice bowls with edible flowers on top—and a vending machine dispenses strawberry swirl ice cream cones wrapped in cardboard. We spend two hours there, unwinding our bodies from the confines of sitting in a car. We buy a *Frozen* headband, I breastfeed M in a pristine nursing pod, and we do some gift shopping.

One Saturday, we get invited to a five-year-old's birthday party, where we get a deeper look into the lives of the elite Tokyo moms in flowy linen dresses. I'm used to American kid birthday parties that take place in public parks where the parents are running around, chasing kids while cutting cake and handing out party favors, and everyone eats cold cheese pizza. This party takes place in a large, rented suite at the top of a high-rise apartment building. A string trio in evening gowns plays classical music while kids run up and down a narrow staircase, throwing balloons across the room and screaming. It is actually very chaotic, but the birthday boy's mom has hired a babysitter to watch the kids while the moms kick back. Kids are all over the place and there are balloons everywhere, but the room is not messy. One mom recognizes me from day care and invites me down to a quiet corner where she and three other impeccably coiffed moms are drinking champagne and chatting. "Join us at the adult section," she says warmly. "You must be tired from looking after your kids." The women are gathered around a long wooden table with dozens of tiny bamboo bento boxes filled with delectable bites of pickled vegetables, tiny pieces of toast with smoked salmon and dill on top, smoked fish, simmered beef and potatoes, and sponge cakes. There is even a real live chef standing behind a grill cooking some of the best steak I have ever eaten. The moms have switched out their weekday linen for silk blouses and fitted white jeans, and they chatter on and on about their plans for the weekend and kids' lessons. They try to gently include me, but I feel like the ugly duckling, and I also find that I cannot let go of watching my children with the same abandon that these moms seem to have. In the first few minutes that we're there, N falls on the staircase and starts crying really loudly. Since then, I'm on high alert to make sure they (or I) don't inadvertently embarrass us or stand out.

Being in Tokyo with the kids, I find myself exaggerating my Japanese mannerisms so that people know I am a good Japanese mom. Alone, I am a middle-aged Japanese woman who blends in well enough with the rest of the fabric of society, seemingly capable of upholding the peace and harmony of my Japanese surroundings. But when I'm with my small mixed-race kids and my Black husband, I suddenly seem more unpredictable, a potential threat to the surrounding peace and quiet. The dependability of

Japan relies on consistency and sameness, which we obviously are not bringing to the table. Everywhere I look in Tokyo, all the moms are pushing the same stroller, carrying their toddlers on the back of the same bicycle in the same toddler bicycle seat, keeping their babies cozy with the same Uniqlo quilted blanket. The lack of diversity is frustrating, and I also start to feel a little left out—like I want to be accepted. To convince people that we are not a threat, I subconsciously find myself overemphasizing my good-Japanese-mom-ness publicly, saying little tedious things to my daughter in Japanese, making shuffling movements, telling her incessantly, *Take your shoes off the seat, don't drink in the taxi, don't run or make loud noises in public.*

Other moms who, like me, are ethnically Japanese but live in other contexts, admit that they feel the same kind of pressure when they're out and about, especially in the cities. "It's much different in the countryside," one mom whose hometown is in rural northern Japan tells me. "People are a lot more tolerant of kids. But in Tokyo, you will definitely get lots of side-eyes from strangers if your kids aren't on their best behavior."

"When I'm back in Japan, I feel like I'm in a fishbowl," a Japanese friend who lives in the United States says.

Says another, "When people look at me in the United States, I assume they're looking at me because they think my child is adorable or they feel loving feelings toward me as a new mom. In Japan, I assume they're silently judging or scrutinizing or waiting for me to screw up."

While I'm shuffling around doing my good-Japanese-mom charade, the real Japanese moms are just sitting around coolly monitoring their kids from a distance. As for the rest of the good citizens of the motherland, they are almost always subtly watching, but like Academic Lady at the café, they seldom say anything or actively intervene. This is not a culture of learn-as-you-go, on-the-job training. The training should be done, and now the kids—and their parents—are being examined, being tested in real time on their performance.

After more than a month here, some of the beautiful unspoken promises we are asked to make to society—no running, no screaming, no spilling—start to feel overbearing and impossible. I feel more tired and cranky than I hope to be on most days. The stifling humidity is much harder to bear with tiny, slow-paced, whiny humans in tow. Navigating Tokyo with a toddler and a stroller in the summer heat is birthing in me a whole new level of exhaustion that I did not expect. Escalators and staircases that make the city so vertically efficient for able-bodied adults are major impediments to stroller manipulation. Everyone raves about the Tokyo train system, but some stations don't have elevators, so if you are traveling with a heavy-duty stroller on public transport, you might have to choose to use a different station that adds tons of time to your commute. This is probably why most Japanese moms either strap their babies to their bodies or teach their toddlers how to be on foot. Only wealthy parents who take taxis everywhere and ignorant nonresidents like me who don't know any better are carrying strollers.

Tokyo has changed a bit since I was growing up there. There are definitely more tourists walking around the city. Signs at stores and train stations are not just in Japanese but in English, Chinese, and Korean, too. I see more mixed-race couples and families walking around neighborhoods than ever before, which gives me hope that—if we ever choose to move back here—my kids will not be ostracized or singled out in the same way that some of my obviously mixed-race friends were when I was growing up. There is a Black Lives Matter Japan movement, as well as numerous podcasts and Instagram influencers discussing issues of diversity and race. It's clear that this generation of Japanese parents is not adopting wholesale the rigorous principles that were passed down to them—instead, they are using their own judgment about what's important and what isn't. Even though it's still nothing compared with the United States, I see more kids running on the streets or talking back to their parents, even in public. But I can also feel the tension in the air in places where old Japanese values are in direct contact with the influx of difference. Large flags alongside the busy streets of Shibuya ask pedestrians in bold English type to keep their voices down while they walk. A small handwritten placard in front of an independent boutique in the hip Daikanyama neighborhood says, in neat block letters, "Dear foreign travelers. We are only open for shopping, not sightseeing." On my way home from work one day, I stop by the Loft department store and go up to the top floor, where there is a tax-free counter for non-residents to get refunds on purchases made at the store. It's like arriving at an airport. Dozens of visitors from many different countries are there, some sitting on the floor, some with their feet up on a wall, most speaking at volumes way louder than the average Japanese. Amid them are half a dozen security guards in little sailor hats and suspenders desperately trying to convince these visitors to stay in a single-file line and not take a seat on the floor. This scene makes me realize how hard it is for the Japanese to enforce their rigid ways in the face of an increasingly globalizing world.

I start to miss the freedom of letting my kid wander around a restaurant without the worry of causing meiwaku. I miss the ease of pulling out my breast in the corner of a restaurant to feed a fussy baby. I get tired of bowing profusely and apologetically every time one of my two foreign-looking children makes a loud noise or puts her feet on the chair, which happens all the time. In America, if you have kids in tow, you get a free pass for your messy hair, your spit-stained shirt, and the loud volume of your table at a restaurant. In Japan, parents—especially moms—are expected to keep things together despite or maybe even especially because of the presence of their offspring. It's a lot of pressure. "I always felt like my kids were super unkempt," Sarah from *The Economist*, who used to frequent parks and indoor play areas in Shibuya with her small kids, says. "[The other moms] have their kids with bows in their hair [and are] super well-dressed, and I would have wet hair and vomit all over me. It was intimidating."

By mid-July, I'm starting to feel the pressure, too. It's hot and I'm feeling ready to go back to California, where I can be in my sweatpants with my hair in a mom bun all day, go everywhere in my car, and not have to worry about how my kids are acting all the time.

SIX

The Care and Feeding of a Japanese-Inspired Child

N and I are sitting at a restaurant table in Shibuya. She has a forlorn look on her face.

"He's not going to wake up," N says, stroking the teddy bear's head lovingly with her soup spoon.

"He wants to go to sleep forever," I tell her. "He's so tired."

"I'm so tired, I want to become a soup," the teddy bear says as he melts into the bowl.

We're at a gimmicky teddy bear–themed restaurant in Shibuya that serves shabu-shabu, a popular dish that consists of beef and vegetables cooked in boiling water and then dipped in flavored broth. Here, the gelatinous broth is frozen into teddy bear shapes. It's not the most delicious food in Japan, but it's the type of place—like the Samurai restaurant in Akihabara and the Ninja restaurant in Ōtemachi—that attracts kids, tourists, and local enthusiasts. Patrons can choose to wear borrowed teddy bear hats and gloves during the meal, or to invite a giant teddy bear stuffie to dine with them at the table. It's the combination of places like this and other creative kids' menus that seems to have changed N's palate from the mostly carb and cheese diet she was starting to adopt in the United States to something more diversified and healthful. Kids' menus in Japanese restaurants have at least four or five different kinds of foods on a plate. They are in small portions, many different colors, and cooked in a way that kids will like, without compromising the flavor of the food itself. The price is typically between five and ten dollars, nothing that breaks the bank. Sometimes it's served on a cute plate—a fire truck or an Anpanman face—and sometimes it comes with a toy or some stickers. During our time in Tokyo, we have lots of colorful meals served in neatly compartmentalized bento boxes. The kids also eat adult food, which is nutritious and delicious and not overseasoned, allowing kids to enjoy the natural flavors of the cuisine. I learn that light soy sauce–based broths, lightly salted fresh vegetables boiled to perfection, the airy crispiness of tempura batter, and the slightly sweet aroma of sushi rice are really kid-friendly, even without being forced to be.

One day, we go to a casual family restaurant that advertises a kids' lunch for 590 yen (five dollars). There are just two options: Lunch A and Lunch B. Lunch A consists of shrimp tempura, two small potato wedges, a golf ball-sized hamburger, a cup of corn soup, a broccoli floret, quarter-sized carrot slices, and a scoop of flavored rice with chicken, peas, and carrots inside. Lunch B is the same lunch, but instead of the chicken rice, you get udon noodles. Each lunch is served on a plate that looks like a car. The textures and colors and shapes of the food, the presentation, the experience of eating itself, is fun and explorative. This simple choice—A or B? Rice or noodles?—gives N a sufficient sense of agency while making sure she gets all her nutrition in one meal. The idea of a kid-friendly restaurant is very different back in the United States, where kids are given crayons and coloring pages to play with before their meal, but the food itself is usually something simple and quite bland, like grilled cheese, mac and cheese, or a quesadilla with cheese. (Kids do love cheese!)

But the best food N eats in Japan is at Tiny Friends, her day care. Every day, these kids eat an incredibly well-balanced five-course meal cooked by three women who wear professional chef's outfits. A weekly menu shows parents how the school is making sure that every day the kids are eating a balance of food that nourishes the brain, food that warms the body, and food that provides comfort. One day the menu consists of rice, red fish grilled in ginger, blanched komatsuna (Japanese mustard spinach), and eggplant and onion miso soup, with a snack of sweet potato butter mochi and milk. The next day, they eat rice and mabo tofu with a minced daikon radish salad and Chinese-style seaweed and scallion soup. The school proudly displays its daily menus—prepared two ways, as a porridge for the little ones and as real meals for toddlers—in a glass case by the front door. Every day, I stop to *ooh* and *aah* at the food display while N explains cheerfully how much she ate. "The soup was soooo good," she says.

Japanese school lunches are governed by a program called shokuiku, or food education. Shokuiku began in the late 1800s when a Buddhist temple in Yamagata prefecture introduced macrobiotic diets to underserved communities via a school food drive. The idea spread throughout the country, with similar programs popping up everywhere. The 1954 School Lunch Program Act further codified the expansion of nutritious lunches and food education in schools. Shokuiku isn't just about eating. A digital leaflet published by the government says this: "School lunches can be thought of as a living textbook, because they involve regional culture and cuisine, along with concepts such as gratitude for everyone involved in the food sector—from production to distribution to consumption. Our initiatives are designed to promote a safe-and-healthy lifestyle." Today's cafeteria meals in Japan are made daily from natural ingredients, either on campus or at a central kitchen in the neighborhood. There are nearly 7,000 nutrition and diet teachers across Japan's forty-seven prefectures who work with families and educators on everything from how to prepare and clean up meals hygienically, to how to reduce food waste by teaching children to recognize the hard work of farmers and suppliers, to what the nutritional elements in the provided meals are. A viral Instagram video of the lunch prep process at a middle school just outside Tokyo shows a team of masked, gloved cafeteria workers who are stirring a giant vat of chicken meatballs with generous amounts of carrots, cabbage, scallions, ginger, and soy sauce in it to make a delicious-looking soup. Everything is made by hand—"even the broth is made from chicken bone and vegetable scraps!"

When I was pregnant with N, my friend Akane gave me a baby shokuiku cookbook published by NHK, a Japanese broadcaster. The book presents an important theory: that lifelong eating habits start the moment a baby has their first taste of real food. "Adults and babies should enjoy the deliciousness of natural ingredients, together," writes the author. The book is full of recipes created by a professional chef using beautiful ingredients like white sesame, dried horse mackerel, and burdock root.

According to the author, there are four stages of babyhood before kids become real eaters:

- The early "gulping" phase, at five to six months of age, when babies start to show interest in food by staring at family members during mealtimes and moving their mouths. He suggests using a mortar and pestle or a citrus juicer to create mushy, diluted versions of everything adults eat.

- The "munch munch" phase, at seven to eight months, when you introduce real foods mushed down to the texture of tofu or flan: carbs to provide energy; fruits and veggies for vitamins and minerals; and protein like meat, fish, and eggs. (But nothing smelly, fibrous, fatty, raw, or chewy.)
- The "bite bite" phase, nine to eleven months, the optimal time to introduce foods that babies can hold themselves. This is also the time to start adding light flavor-enhancing agents like soy sauce, miso, ketchup, and mayonnaise.
- The "chomp chomp" phase at twelve to fifteen months, when kids are growing real teeth and developing bacteria in their mouths. This is when they can have real foods like fish and meat. It's also the time to let them experiment with cutlery, and use animal shapes, colors, and other things they recognize to help them understand the diversity of food.

With my first kid, I was too overwhelmed with parenting and the pandemic to even open this book. It isn't until M is born that I pull it down from the bookshelf. Second-time parenting is a whole other ball game. I am more confident. More at ease, even though with two children, my life is much more chaotic. I decide to try to raise M on shokuiku. It's a long-term experiment to see if she will develop taste buds now that deter her from wanting only mac and cheese and rice when she's N's age.

Kids know only what they know. If they grow up being fed mac and cheese and french fries, they will probably grow up to love mac and cheese and french fries. If they grow up eating homemade burdock, pounded into a gentle mash with soft stewed white rice with a stone-hearthed mortar and pestle, then maybe they will grow to love that, too. N loves natto, stinky fermented soybeans. A vast majority of my friends who didn't grow up eating it don't learn to love it. It's one of those things that we typically consider an acquired taste.

My first experiment is boiled cabbage mashed up with homemade dashi broth. The dashi is made of kombu and bonito. As instructed, I put a ten-centimeter square of kombu in a liter of water and bring it to a near-boil, at which point I remove the kombu with a pair of tongs and put it in the compost. I rummage through my cutlery drawer and find a purple plastic spoon, a tiny wooden spoon that came with some fancy loose-leaf tea, and a child-sized silver spoon that my mom bought for N when she was born. One of these spoons has to work. M is making all the signs of being ready for the gulping phase. She always wakes up when we are having a meal, wailing to signal that she wants to be at the table, even though she can't hold herself up yet. She makes funny munching motions with her lips when I bring anything close to her mouth, whether that's food or a finger. The cabbage is a hit. The crunch usually associated with this common cruficerous vegetable has been reduced to a translucent pale green, refreshing mulch combined with the dashi that she seems to not mind at all. In a matter of seconds this thirteen-pound baby has devoured approximately one entire leaf. A clear winner.

Next, I try the red snapper stew. A slightly more complicated preparation, this recipe calls for the raw fish to be doused in salt for thirty minutes, then cooked lightly in boiling water until the skin comes off, then steamed along with some asparagus and a shiitake mushroom. For "gulping" babies, the chef recommends taking a small amount of fish and a single cut of asparagus, and putting it in the mortar and pestle along with the base dashi from earlier. I mash everything up into a textured fish stew. This doesn't go so well. M starts crying, and when she cries, I see a bunch of white fish flakes stuck to the roof of her mouth. She eventually swallows it, but I won't be trying it again.

I tell M's nanny at the time, who is from West Africa like Hubby, about my food experiments. "Look," I say somewhat proudly, "I made her some more food. This is grated daikon radish in this dashi sauce that the chef from this book recommended."

She makes a face. "This doesn't look appetizing," she says. "She's gonna end up hating food." But M doesn't hate food. In fact, she tries pretty much anything.

The bento is the ultimate expression of Japanese maternal love. A 2010 television commercial created by the mega ad agency

Dentsu for Tokyo Gas, the gas provider in our capital, shows a mom who can communicate with her growing son only through her lunch-making. Every day, she makes him a bento representing her sentiments toward her growing child: a box full of veggies to wish him good health; a colorful chirashi sushi plate with a smiley face made with edamame to cheer him up; a bed of rice with a heart to congratulate him on a new girlfriend. "My son's only reply was always an empty bento box," she says. For his final bento, presumably before he goes to college, he finally responds with a simple note in the empty container: "I'm sorry I haven't been able to say thank you all this time."

In a culture where a verbal "I love you" or even hugging a parent are not the norm, creating beautiful food for other people is a love language that Japanese people have become quite fluent in. Japanese supermarkets and department stores have an extensive selection of bento and precooked baby food. Sometimes they come in a simple box with compartments to keep the flavors from bleeding into one another. Sometimes they come in stacked boxes to give the semblance of a multicourse meal. Sometimes they are wrapped in delicate cotton cloth. Bento photos have become a major internet phenomenon, and there are even coffee-table books featuring expertly designed lunches made by Japanese moms. Supermarket baby food is categorized by brand and age. The options include things like chicken liver and vegetable stew; white fish in cream sauce; pasta with Hokkaido corn; simmered beef, potatoes, and carrots; rice with seaweed, daikon radish, and bluefin tuna. All of them are prepared so they can be eaten inside the container they're sold in.

My friend Satomi—the same one who makes the awesome mom bag—makes the cutest bento lunches for her daughter Mia. She doesn't just cut blocks of cheese to put inside; she buys tiny cheese balls with the Anpanman character on them. Her vegetables are simmered and stewed with dashi and come with a tiny little homemade condiment dispenser made of plastic wrap. She ties the plastic wrap with a rubber band and pokes a hole in the purse using a toothpick. When Mia squeezes the plastic, a sliver of mayonnaise comes out. "My mom used to do this for me," Satomi explains. "So now I do it in my bento boxes. It brings the kids a tiny bit of joy and it keeps the rest of the food from getting soggy." A tiny, loving mayonnaise squeeze trick, passed down from generation to generation. For Satomi, cute bento lunch prep is an extension of a much more involved dinner program. Not unlike in the preschool N went to in Japan, she designs the week's menu in advance—always a combination of a protein, two vegetable dishes, and a starch. Over coffee one morning in Berkeley, she shares her family menu for the week with me. Miso-flavored fish croquettes, corn and cucumber, sweet potato soup. Simmered beef bowl with avocado and tomato, egg pasta with corn soup, chicken and egg bowl with seaweed soup. Lazy rice. (Lazy rice, she tells me, is frozen rice that can be easily reheated on days when she doesn't have a lot of time to cook.) Satomi learned how to cook by watching her mom, and she knows she doesn't have to hold herself to these standards, but she likes it. She wants her kids to have what she had growing up. Her kids, as a result, eat pretty much anything their mom cooks for them. They come home asking excitedly, "What's for dinner?" and finish everything on their plates. Which surprises nobody, I'm sure—I mean, I would, too.

At a playdate at another CB family's house, I stand uselessly in the kitchen as Maki, the mom, elegantly prepares an impromptu dinner for five kids and three adults with her one-and-a-half-year-old son clinging to one leg. She deftly chops up some mushrooms, sautés them with beef and broccoli, pulls crispy nori seaweed brought directly from Japan out of the freezer ("The stuff they sell here is expensive and tastes bad!"), cuts some baby tomatoes in half, and places them on five melamine plates. Then, she takes freshly cooked koshihikari rice specially grown and harvested at a farm in Sacramento from her Zojirushi rice cooker (it's a high-end exclusive-to-Japan model that her husband hand-carried on a recent flight back), puts it in a bowl, and mixes it up with sesame seeds and grilled marinated salmon flakes. She gives me a little bowl of this very special rice and salmon dish. "The kids love it," she tells me.

"Did you make it yourself?" I ask her.

"Of course, of course!" she says. "Have some!" I manage to spoon a small morsel of this aromatic rice dish into my mouth before the baby clinging to her leg catches on and starts asking for bites, and I feed him the rest. We have a delicious dinner together, and then, of course, she creates a little bento box for her school-aged kids to take with them the next day. After we finish eating, she wipes down each kid's chair with a nontoxic cleaning spray. "Their hands are so sticky!" she says, as if she needs an excuse for her meticulousness.

Today, Japanese bento boxes have gone beyond the boundaries of the island nation and become a global pastime for parents who want to bring joy to their kids. Eating the colors of the rainbow is a practice I've heard many families partake in no matter where they are in the world, and new ingredients are being introduced to children's diets every day.

Mayumi Uejiima-Carr lives in San Diego and runs the US division of global food advocacy nonprofit TABLE FOR TWO. While most Table for Two activities focus on food access in Asia and Africa, the US-based program also combats obesity and unhealthful eating through an interactive Japanese-inspired food education program for schools across the country. "Many schools in the US serve meals that rely on frozen and processed foods with additives, in part due to limited budgets and infrastructure," Mayumi tells me. Many American public schools don't have sufficient resources to teach a lot about food or cooking. They are governed by nutrition standards, but there is often limited emphasis on flavor, presentation, or overall appeal of the food. There is real data showing that more healthful school meals with less additives and sugar lead to better academic outcomes and focus. When the TABLE FOR TWO USA team shows up at schools with tools and tips on how to make sushi or okonomiyaki from scratch, the kids soak it up. "When the learning curve is from zero to one, the impact is pretty big." Mayumi has two kids of her own with whom she sometimes prepares meals to teach them how to appreciate cooking and eating. "We make onigiri with salmon, a tamagoyaki egg roll, maybe put a tomato and cucumbers on the side. . . . Then we examine all the colors on our plate: white, pink, yellow, red, green! And maybe add a sprinkle of furikake (Japanese rice seasoning)."

Because my husband's a chef and I'm a full-time working person, most of the time I'm not the one who makes my kids' meals or prepares their bento. When I do, though, that's when my inner Japanese mom really comes to life. I go to Daiso one afternoon and purchase a handful of cheap trinkets that will help amplify my Japanese mom chops—vegetable cutters shaped like flowers and hearts and stars; little plastic toothpicks with tiny smiling carrots and tomatoes perched on top; pink flower-covered doilies for putting side dishes on; plastic rice molds shaped like dolphins, bunnies, and daisies. Whenever it's my turn to make their bento, I bust out my collection of heart- and star-shaped cookie cutters, drop some white rice into my trusty Zojirushi rice cooker, and scope the fridge for some simple protein and veggies and fruits. N and M each get a bed of rice with purple shiso-flake sprinkles, heart-shaped omelets nestled on top and some bright orange ikura salmon roe sprinkled on top of that, and a side of baby tomatoes cut in half with the carrot toothpicks perched on them. "Happy birthday!" N exclaims when I show her the colorful bento box. Coming from N, this is the ultimate compliment. The kid loves birthdays more than anything in the whole world. For dinner, I use a flower mold to create petals of rice and in the center put some creamy stew with cauliflower, chicken, and carrots. This is *not* the same as the level of attention to detail and care that a real Japanese mom in Japan might put into bento-making. But I understand the joy of doing this. And I'm into it.

It's no secret that Tokyo is one of the best culinary cities in the world. Japan has more Michelin stars than any other country, and chefs from every corner of this earth come here to train and learn the secrets of the cuisine. The famed Danish restaurant Noma did a pop-up in Kyoto in the summer of 2023; in advance of that, its chef-owner René Redzepi brought his entire team with him for a ten-week residency where they explored the tools, techniques, and craftsmanship behind Japanese cuisine. The late Anthony Bourdain once said, "If I were trapped in one city and had to eat one nation's cuisine for the rest of my life, I would not mind eating Japanese."

Enjoying delicious food is innate in humans. If we believe that kids are just big humans in training, it naturally makes sense that we'd also train them to love food and know how to appreciate fine flavors and good ingredients. I'm not patient enough—or in the kitchen often enough—to cook with my kids all the time, but I do try to have DIY meal events with the girls whenever I can so that they can learn about timeless techniques and ingredients that make our cultures and the food we eat. "We should cook with them, instead of plopping them in front of the TV to watch Mickey Mouse while we make their food," I say to Hubby. "Bonding over cooking is a great way to connect more deeply with them and make sure they don't end up being finnicky eaters!"

This is what I tell myself on one solo parenting weekend, when I spend hours procuring and preparing materials for a sushi-making party—crisp nori seaweed, sweet tamagoyaki omelets, imitation crab, pickled burdock and cucumbers cut into thin strips, a couple of bamboo rolling mats—only to discover that the kids just want to eat natto with plain white rice. It's still hit or miss whether they'll eat what they make, but the experience also matters . . . right?

SEVEN

Who Wants to Be a Japanese Mom, Anyway?

In Japan, parenting *actually* comes with a user manual. It's called the boshi techo (maternity planner), and it comes in the form of an A5-size, eighty-four page, softcover booklet. As soon as I inform the Japanese Consulate that I'm pregnant, they send me my very own copy of the boshi techo. It's a manual for moms and babies that every expecting Japanese mom gets from their local government. The boshi techo has step-by-step instructions on how we should think, act, and behave from the moment we find out we're pregnant and throughout the child's life, from birth all the way to age twenty. Like most things Japanese, it is irritatingly pedantic and incredibly useful. Building a harmonious society doesn't just magically happen. It's a team effort, a public-private partnership with strict rules, clear messaging, and lots of reinforcement mechanisms—starting with this innocuous booklet.

The first section of the boshi techo is a play-by-play of what happens during every month of pregnancy. It gives detailed advice on things like what to eat, when to start thinking about naming your child, and how to ask for attention when everyone around you starts to hyperfocus on the impending baby. After that, there's a whole section packed with medical advice and worksheets to document pregnancy health, dental health, mental health, postpartum health, and the baby's health.

Then the booklet transitions to the early stages of parenting, where the advice turns super specific—and also a little random. The booklet details what parents should be doing at every stage of their children's development so that they grow up to be good citizens of society: "Look your baby in the face and talk and play with him or her," it suggests to moms of newborns. Then, about one year in: "Your child will begin to enjoy scribbling with crayons or creating some sort of meaning out of wooden blocks or toy bricks. You should try to play together at these times." During the "terrible twos," the booklet tells parents, "Both mother and father should hold and hug your child with a smile. Your child will become picky, self-assertive, or make selfish demands. Instead of refusing outright, first listen, then respond in a kind manner." There's even advice for dads, like "You should be kind to your wife, encourage her, and be proactive in performing household chores" and "The father should also have close physical contact with the baby, and should provide help, even if at first he is just changing diapers or giving a bath." My first impression is: I like this! There's something really comforting about having advice every step of the way, like having a best friend or a chatbot that knows exactly what you're going through. Maybe this is why Japanese moms, even the ones who are hauling multiple kids around, don't look like they're freaking out at all about the little creatures they are responsible for keeping alive.

Local resource centers offer an array of booklets for parents—including a manual on what to do when your child throws up, a natural disaster preparedness guide for families with kids, and a catalog published by the local library suggesting age-appropriate books for kids newborn to six. Each booklet is filled with colorful illustrations, thoughtful explanations, and QR codes that link to sites where you can download useful apps or buy necessary materials, like a ready-to-go emergency kit or enough freeze-dried food for a family of four to survive for three days.

Here are some baby milestones for the first year of life from historical education publishing company Benesse's *Brand New! First Child-Rearing Encyclopedia*, which I picked up at a neighborhood resource center:

0–6 MONTHS:

Teach them the joy of aisatsu (proper Japanese greetings).

Start saying good morning and good night, making proper eye contact.

7 MONTHS:

Show them how to wash their hands.

Show them how to wave "hello" and "goodbye" to adults.

AGE 1:

Teach them how to change their clothes.

Show them how to clean up after themselves.

Practice gargling.

Even mass retailers participate in the education and micromanagement of a Japanese mom. The baby superstore Akachan Honpo has the square footage of a Costco, but walking through its aisles is almost the opposite experience. The lighting is pleasant, and the store is pin-drop quiet, aside from the pleasant background music interspersed with occasional announcements about the latest sale on diapers. A padded bench thoughtfully surrounds the supporting beams, doubling as a place for tired shoppers to rest and a bulletin board for promotions and sales and free parent education materials. The day I visit, the store is full of young moms in flowy linen summer dresses, some with their husbands and others with their parents, all pushing brand new strollers, weaving up and down the pristine aisles. I float through the maternity section, which is filled with the exact same outfit that the moms walking around are wearing, in six different shades of neutral beiges and pinks. A huge corner of the store is dedicated to parents taking care of baby needs: half a dozen padded changing stations are lined up next to one another, and a nursing area hides behind a "women only" sign, offering little makeshift stalls, each with a comfy chair and table, separated by simple brown curtains. A scale and tape measure are readily available so you can measure your baby and then shop for the right size.

Akachan Honpo doesn't just sell products; it's a resource for young parents and parents-to-be. The company does extensive research on the behaviors of new parents and publishes them. For example, they report that the average Japanese household uses 19.8 baby wipes a day at birth, with more than a third using a single wipe without folding, another third folding a single wipe in half, and a smaller percentage using two wipes. This type of data might seem useless to the public, but let's be honest: We all wonder if our little behaviors, our ways of thinking, are "normal" or "correct"—especially when we're doing things for the first time. I admit that I have wondered about these seemingly trivial things, like how many wipes I should use every time I change my baby. Sometimes, in an effort to save wipes, I even rip them in half and stuff the unused half back in the box. Knowing that the average household uses twenty makes me feel better that I'm on the right side of the wipe-conservation effort. When I'm in California, it doesn't feel as important to be doing things the same way as everyone else. In Japan, because it's such a unified community with set standards, it does. There's a sense of comfort in knowing you did things right, or at least that you're not a disparaging anomaly from the rest of society.

It's easy for me to exoticize Japanese momming based on my intermittent visits back home. As a person living in America, I'm subjected to very few "shoulds" on the day to day. In the United States, it's okay for moms to go outside with uncombed hair hidden under a baseball cap and kids with frosting smeared across their face. Many of us are in our mid-forties, simultaneously lugging around toddlers while working through issues like worsening eyesight and perimenopause.

But the truth is, Japanese momming is a job that's becoming less and less desirable. More and more Japanese women, especially of the younger generation, are rejecting marriage and parenthood. They don't want to be told what to do. Of all the shoulds and structures and systems that make Japan so organized and great, the institution of motherhood is, perhaps, in the most perilous state. Mom candidates don't want to mom anymore. This is a serious problem! Birth rates in Japan have been on a steady decline, but 2024 was a record-breaking year with the lowest in recorded history. Hiroshi Yoshida, a professor at Tohoku University's Research Center for Aged Economy and Society, predicts that at this rate, only one child younger than the age of fourteen will remain in the country by the year 2720. He's sort of joking, of course, but the fact that this is statistically plausible should put us on high alert.

In a survey conducted by the nonprofit grantmaker Nippon Foundation in 2023, only 17 percent of seventeen-to-nineteen-year-olds said with certainty that they wanted to get married and have kids. The popular teen shopping mall Shibuya 109 found that 33 percent of fifteen-to-twenty-four-year-olds don't want to have kids at all, while 50 percent said they wanted to have kids only if they could also keep working. A lot of younger Japanese women believe that a childless life means more financial freedom, better career options, and less things to worry about. "In today's Japan, there's no guarantee that we can make our kids happy," one mom says. "I would feel irresponsible bringing a child into these circumstances."

While all of society participates in supporting the growth and well-being of Japanese children, it's the mom who is at the core of it all, doing a lot of the invisible labor of parenting—managing household logistics, taking kids to baby classes, keeping the home front tidy and the kids in check. The feminist in me cringes at how overgeneralizing it sounds to speak about societal roles so determined by gender. But let's be real: Japanese society is still deeply sexist. You can't ignore it. "Even a woman can easily fold this up on the go!" boasts an online ad for a lightweight stroller. "This TV is easy to set up, even for a woman," a kind older salesman at an electronics store says to me when I accompany my parents to buy a new TV. "The ladies' set is a lighter portion, perfect for women!" a poster featuring a seasonal menu for a popular lunch spot declares. Everywhere I turn, there are subtle suggestions that women are weaker, smaller, and less capable of complex tasks.

Part of the problem is that working while momming is really a bleak prospect for most Japanese women—and has been for a long time. Despite the first wave of global feminism in the 1980s and the workplace policy reforms that followed, Japan is still a highly patriarchal society with both explicit and implicit expectations around things like when to get married and have children, how to maintain a household, and how to raise kids. When I was growing up, a Japanese woman who was not married at the age of twenty-five was called a Christmas cake—a seasonal item whose value plummets exponentially if it's not snatched up before its expiration date. A woman who wasn't married by thirty was dubbed a loser dog. These tropes have faded out, but the ripple effects still exist. A lot of young Japanese people still engage in the practice of konkatsu—the active search for a marriage partner—with the goal of getting married before the age of thirty. After marriage, it's still largely assumed that women will have kids before the age of thirty-five, before their fertility drops. You don't legally qualify for IVF or sperm donation if you are not part of a married couple (or a couple that is living together and planning to get married). It's not easy to get donors and surrogates, and egg freezing for future use is also not an option. Only a man and a woman can legally marry in Japan, so same-sex couples have to jump through many hoops if they want to have kids.

Once married, a couple must take the same last name and create their own family register, an official document under Japanese family law that certifies the identity and family relationships of

Japanese citizens. The vast majority of the time, the woman takes the man's last name. "This means women often have to update all their personal identification materials, even at work," Fumino Sugiyama, an LGBTQ+ activist who has been fighting for the right for married couples to have different last names, tells me. "For professionals like doctors and researchers, changing their name can be particularly complicated because it impacts their work history and academic publications." The folks fighting at the opposite end of this debate argue that allowing individuals to maintain their premarital surnames could break the sanctity of the family structure. Despite some decades of dialogue around this issue, a clear path to change is still not on the horizon.

Japan famously grew its post–World War II economy by adopting a hyper-disciplined workforce culture consisting of long hours, a strict hierarchy of yes-men, and almost no women in positions of power. Companies like Toyota and Sony were being built from scratch by men who worked their butts off while their wives stayed at home and took care of the children. The men are called salarymen; they are the workforce largely responsible for the decades of rapid economic growth for which Japan became so famous. The stereotypical Japanese salaryman works in a corporate office and professes undying, lifelong loyalty to the firm and sells his soul to the company, its leader, and its norms. His worth is measured in how hard he can drive himself without breaking. His purpose in life is the same as the company's purpose. He's a 100 percent devoted servant of the workplace. In the late 1980s, at the height of the bubble economy, the pharmaceutical company Sankyo launched an energy drink called Regain and ran a promotional campaign with a series of short, catchy commercials featuring a heroic military-esque tune sung by a Japanese businessman, played by the actor Saburō Tokitō. The commercials featured Tokitō dressed in a suit boarding a plane to a tropical destination, rowing a boat in Venice, barreling down a busy road in a samurai outfit, singing, "Can you fight for twenty-four hours? Like a Japanese businessman!" The song "Signs of Courage"—a catchy tune originally designed for a TV commercial—sold more than 600,000 copies. Even today, an estimated one-third of working people in Japan qualify as salarymen. Japan has a long history of uncontested top-down rulers. In the hit Hulu show *Shōgun*, there's an undeniable leader and an endless troop of people who sacrifice their lives beneath him. This type of system, though formally abolished, has continued for a long time, with people working relentlessly even when it costs them their health (if that's what the leader wants). In the 2010s, in response to a few highly publicized instances of death from overwork, the Japanese government implemented a nationwide workplace reform effort that included measures like allowing more people to work remotely and banning forced overtime. It's been somewhat effective, but the hierarchical workplace vibe is still very much present.

The counterpart to the martyrlike salaryman was the sengyo shufu—a role *The Japan Times*, Japan's leading English-language newspaper, describes as "a woman with no independent income who sticks to being a housewife." While the salaryman was out dedicating his life to his job, his wife was expected to have kids and become a full-time professional homemaker. Sometimes the family would move in with the husband's parents and the wife would be expected to take care of multiple generations, working under the rule of her mother-in-law. (Of course, the idea of a woman staying home to take care of the kids is not unique to Japan.) For a long time, there was very little resistance to this expectation. The Japanese language even blatantly reflects this philosophy: The word for wife is *okusan*—the person in the back. There's another more-humble-form word, *kanai*—the person inside the house. In contrast, the word for husband is *shujin*—the main person.

In 1985, Japan passed an equal employment act, and more women entered the workforce, albeit still in roles and at salaries much less significant than men's. The term *OL* (a cringeworthy abbreviation for "office lady") was very widely used to describe a woman who worked in a corporate office serving tea and sending faxes. Companies hired OLs in huge numbers—by the late 1980s, a third of women who worked in Japan were office ladies. These working women were expected to quit their jobs after they got married—and before they had children. It was not, by any stretch of the imagination, a career path.

Until recently, it was totally normal for women to be asked whether they plan to have children during a hiring interview. This practice is now illegal, but most workplaces are still led by the same generation of men who sincerely believe women can't understand the merits of their hardcore salaryman spirit. Despite some policy changes that allow women more opportunity and autonomy in the workplace, the social systems surrounding them haven't changed—and neither have the perceptions and assumptions of their bosses. In reality things are not much better. The return-to-work rate of new moms in Japan is bleak—a staggering 70 percent of women still quit working after giving birth to their first child.

"I actually think it's more challenging to be a Japanese mom today than ever before," Fumino says. "Today's women have to juggle work, housework, and child-rearing all at once. They still face significant biases and gender gaps at work, and they're also being told that their children would be happier if they stayed at home." Fumino, who is transgender, has the unique perspective of being both a Japanese dad and a confidant to many of his childhood besties, many of whom are now Japanese momming. "Some of my most talented and ambitious childhood girlfriends ended up becoming sengyo shufu who had no choice but to take on that role, and as a result, became financially dependent on their husbands," he says. "Seeing them under-stimulated and lost in boredom feels like such a waste."

When you dig one layer deeper into the origins of these patriarchal beliefs, you arrive at the scientific research findings of British psychiatrist John Bowlby. In the early 1950s, Bowlby wrote a series of reports about the role of attachment in child development. Bowlby is credited with being the founder of attachment theory, often used by modern-day therapists to describe how people connect with one another in personal relationships. An attachment style is developed during childhood based on your relationship with your primary caregivers and has lasting effects on how you relate interpersonally with other humans, especially significant others and offspring. His initial research was based on a study he did of poor children who stole things during World War II. He found that a disproportionate number of these delinquent children had experienced prolonged separation from their main caregiver at a very young age. Bowlby published a World Health Organization report based on his findings, and after that, many seemingly credible portals of information—including lots of media and official sources—have latched on to this idea that most of the important development in the brain happens between birth and age three. The "myth of three" was born and spread throughout the world. Today, many experts are disputing the science behind this idea, but it took root even in places as far away as Japan and has proved difficult to undo. The Japanese interpreted Bowlby's findings to mean that birthing mothers must stay at home and focus on child-rearing until the kids are at least three years old. Like all loosely held ideas in Japanese society, this quickly evolved from a suggestion to a rigorously enforced social norm.

"Have you failed as a parent if you're dropping your kid off at day care from Age 0?" a headline for a popular YouTube video asks. Curious, I click Play. The screen cuts to a conference room with fifty participants, mostly women, and an older Japanese man who used to be the head of education in a prefecture on the outskirts of Tokyo. The man is waving his arms and speaking out angrily against the idea of infants going to day care. "Even the UN Declaration on the Rights of the Child says that kids have the right to know and be with their parents!" he shouts at a room full of bewildered moms. "Use your brain! Use your common sense! Of course, a baby of zero, one, two years old wants to be with their mom."

Then, the screen cuts to interviews with some of the moms who are in the audience. "If I think of it as just three years out of my entire life, maybe it's fine. . . . It's just going to be this super-intense time in my life," one mom says. A survey conducted by the Japanese baby product company Pigeon found that 44 percent of Japanese moms still believe that children should be with their mothers until they reach the age of three.

According to the World Economic Forum's 2024 Global Gender Gap Report, Japan's gender parity in economic participation and opportunity is among the lowest in the world (ranking 120th). Japan has the lowest share of senior leadership roles in the entire region of East Asia and the Pacific (14 percent). Only 10 percent of its parliamentary positions and 8.3 percent of ministerial positions are held by women. The government has announced a target of 30 percent female representation in executive positions by 2030, but as of 2024, women occupied just 16.8 percent of executive positions at listed companies in Japan.

Some Japanese politicians are having a hard time coming up with a stance on how to solve the aging population issue. Former Finance Minister Tarō Asō publicly blamed the country's high median age on women who opt out of motherhood. "Some strange people say the aged are to blame, but they are mistaken," Asō, who is older than Joe Biden, said. "The bigger problem lies with those who decide not to give birth to children." One conservative Japanese politician who isn't even worthy of being named in this book suggested on national TV that women should not be allowed to go to college after age eighteen, should be pressured into early childbirth by being unable to marry after twenty-five, and should be given hysterectomies after age thirty. "We need to transform our social structure," he said as a female news anchor side-eyed him hard.

Technically, men can do everything women can do, aside from birthing a child. Dads can change diapers, bathe children, feed kids and clean up after them, run them through a bedtime routine, and still be standing at the end of the day. A study conducted by Darby Saxbe at the University of Southern California Department of Psychology in 2011 found that women's cortisol levels were better when their husbands spent more time doing housework. Healthy cortisol profiles are associated with better marriage outcomes for couples and better health outcomes for women. "Dividing up your housework fairly with your partner may be as important as eating your vegetables," says Saxbe.

And yet, even my most progressive guy friends in Tokyo more often than not have more traditional structures back home. "My wife hasn't gone out with her friends in years," one friend tells me without a hint of apology. "This is what she's always wanted . . . to be a mom. She is really dedicated to her kids."

Ivy League–educated, American-living Japanese dads have said things to me like, "Child-rearing is so hard. It's seriously the hardest time! I mean, I wasn't around much when the kids were little because I was working late until after they were asleep and only saw them briefly before they went to school. But it's so hard!" And "I get what you're going through. . . . I understand. I've watched my wife do all the things you're doing now." A Japanese male friend of mine became a new dad recently, but he didn't take parental leave because he didn't believe he could be helpful to his wife. Instead, he made arrangements for the new-mom-to-be to go back to her parents' home in the countryside, where she could get assistance from her own mother. (There is a long-standing tradition of women going back to their home of origin to birth and take care of their newborns. This serves a few purposes: They get some built-in help from their own moms, but it also allows the dad to keep working uninterrupted during the most fragile early moments of their child's life. The practice has been declining in popularity, but according to a couple of different surveys, even today a little over half of Japanese birthing moms go back to their parents' homes for extended stays before, during, or after a baby's birth.)

The Japanese dads of this era want to spend more time with their kids. They don't want to work like the salarymen of their dads' generation. Because the cost of living is getting higher, an increasing number of families are double-income households with two working parents, and that means dads have to chip in to do more of the childcare, too. According to one survey, in 2005, only 50 percent of dads professed to helping at all with raising children. Takami, a Japanese mom who has an eight-year-old boy and a five-year-old girl, works as a massage therapist while her husband is a work-from-home software engineer. "During the COVID pandemic, my husband's job became mostly remote," she tells me. "So now he does all the school drop-offs and pickups, and if there's an emergency with one of the kids, the school has his number, not mine." My Tokyo-based friend Seiko lives upstairs from a day care center in Japan and observes that roughly half the pickups are being done by dads these days.

The government is trying to encourage more dads to take leave so they can participate more proactively in child-rearing, but it's an uphill battle. Today, only 17 percent of Japanese dads take parental leave. Some male employees tell me that although some of their colleagues have taken paternity leave, depending on the workplace culture it is still seen as an unnecessary luxury, something that makes them seem "too soft."

There's a magazine sitting on my bedside table. On the cover is a cartoon drawing of a woman in a green sweatshirt and gray pants passed out flat on the ground next to a baby in a yellow onesie and an orange teddy bear. "Moms, Take a Break from Momming!" the headline begs. In the pages that follow, experts offer advice on how moms can relax a bit on some of the strict rules of parenting. "If you're too tired to change a diaper, it's okay—as long as it isn't poopy." And "It's okay to create one-pot dinner meals so you don't have to wash as many dishes!" It's just as pedantic as any other Japanese reading material, but at least it's telling moms to take a break from overdoing it. One two-page spread is dedicated to "relaxing recipes" (they actually look way more sophisticated than anything I make for my kids), and another is titled "I'm Currently on Break from Momming!" and shares tips from readers on how find a little R & R in their day. "I lean deep into K-pop fangirl-ing, finding like-minded friends online and even traveling to see them," writes a mom of two girls.

"When I don't feel like cooking, I just declare it, and we go out to eat," writes the mom of an eleven-year-old boy.

"On those days that felt impossible," writes another, whose kids are now grown. "I'd take my kids to the convenience store and we'd each buy what we wanted. Onigiri, flan, pastries, all was fair game—the most important message for that moment was that I am off duty. Once we got home, I'd throw a picnic mat on the balcony and watch my kids from the corner of my eye while I drank a beer. I will always remember that feeling, like I was finally catching my breath."

Moms practicing self-care in Japan is a relatively new idea, but it's catching on quickly. "I've heard of a lot of younger moms who take weekend trips to an onsen (a hot spring) with their girlfriends," one Gen X mom tells me.

"There was even one mom from my child's preschool who went overseas by herself, leaving her kids in the care of someone else!" another woman exclaims.

I pretend to be surprised. "Who did she leave her kids with?" I ask with genuine curiosity.

She opens her eyes wide. "Her husband!"

I don't mention that I leave my kids with my husband about once every three months for a week at a time.

In Japan, the American-style cottage industry of nannies and babysitters doesn't exist. The idea that a nonprofessional stranger would be just as capable of nurturing and caring for your child is still very out of left field for many Japanese, and people often live far away from work or in smaller homes, making home-based childcare challenging. When I tell my friend Maho that my nine-month-old goes out with a nanny every day, she raises her eyebrows in not-so-subtle alarm. "You trust your nanny that much? How did you find her? Is she a family member or something?" Maho is a single working mom with three kids. Her kids are older and in school now, but even when they were tiny, she never used a nanny or a babysitter. In fact, she can't really understand the mindset of a parent who would. I tell her I found the nanny online through a childcare app that works similarly to a dating app. "That's unthinkable," she says. "I can't imagine. How?!" Another working mom friend had a babysitter pick up her kids from school, but they took the bus, which was much more reassuring to her than having them in a private vehicle. "At least on the bus there are other people around to make sure everything is safe," she explains. Japan has a solid system of government-approved day care centers, where only qualified childcare providers work. It's free for residents and open until 6:00 p.m., when parents can reasonably leave work. In 2022, only 2.3 percent of households in Japan were using babysitters at all. (In the United States, it's about 13 percent.)

Even in the United States, there's still a significant gap in the amount of work moms typically do versus dads, but from what I can see, American non-birthing partners do help out a lot more than most Japanese dads. In my own household, the more stereotypically "feminine" tasks like cooking meals and putting the kids to bed are done by Hubby, whereas the more "masculine" role of being out all day at a full-time job is conducted by me. As I'm sitting here typing this sentence, it's Hubby who is reading our two girls their bedtime story—something about a moose and a pollywog. He's the one who baby M turns to for comfort when she's having a hard time falling asleep or accidentally smashes her finger in the shower room door. Most of my Japanese mom friends in America take no issue with leaving kids with their dads for several hours, or even days. Every three months or so, the moms from CB organize a night out without our kids and husbands. We reserve a big table at a nearby restaurant and drink wine and talk about whatever is on our minds. Most of us have used babysitters or nannies at least once, if not regularly, to ease the pain of constant parenting.

Newer parenting books emphasize the perspective that there is actually no normal or correct way to do anything. "Just because your shoes aren't lined up perfectly doesn't mean you're going to die," advises a book comedically titled *The World's Most Useless Parenting Book*. "No matter how much stuff you have, if the parents aren't happy then you can't be ready for anything." Another book I picked up called *The Art of Captivating Children's Hearts* advises parents to be more open with their feelings. "The more you use your muscles, the stronger they get," writes Yoshio Kojima, a comedian who specializes in skits geared toward kids. "Feelings are the same. The more you praise others, the stronger your praising power will get . . . by contrast, the more you criticize, the stronger your criticizing power will get."

In today's Japan, few women want to dedicate 100 percent of their lives to kids. The sengyo shufus of the world are dissatisfied, and angry, and wanting more. "The number of people who believe that everything must fit into a rigid mold is slowly decreasing," a mom who works in the baby product industry tells me. "Personal parenting styles are more accepted today than ever before. In the past, doing certain things would have automatically earned you a label of being a 'bad mother,' but now people look at all different scenarios and think, 'Oh yeah, I can see that as a possibility.'"

Whether you're in Japan or America or anywhere else in the world, the reality is this:

While tips and advice from other people or the institutions around us can be helpful, parenting is actually extremely personal. We all want the freedom to choose how to raise our kids. We all want to do it right—and we probably all have very different ideas about what that looks like. There can't be one single way. Knowing this, how can we retain and pass on some of the beautiful traditions and wisdom without taking away the agency of the modern parent?

EIGHT

Japanese Parenting in America

We return to America during the last week of July. The crisp California air and the panoramic views of the Diablo Mountains, the Pacific Ocean, and cityscapes along the bay are a visceral reminder of why I live here. The rest of the family sleeps in, but I'm up with jet lag at the crack of dawn, so I hop in my car and drive down to the Sunday farmers' market. I get out and immediately feel a little bit of culture shock. Half the people wandering around are still in their pajamas, looking like they just rolled out of bed. Everybody is super open and friendly, even to people they don't know. In Japan, commenting on people's things or appearance would be straight-up off-putting and rude, but here it's an expected part of the community vibe.

"I love your hair!" the pastry shop lady remarks as someone walks by.

"Ohh, what beautiful flowers!" the man selling vegetables says to a patron.

People of all skin tones and age ranges are buying oversized bushels of leafy greens and baskets of mixed berries from market stalls lined up next to one another in no particular order. A bunch of kids of all sizes are running around a scraggly creek while a white man in a bowler hat and Thai fisherman pants strums a guitar and sings a folk song next to a rotisserie chicken truck. All over the market, people are laughing with their mouths wide open, something you almost never see in Japan, where laughter is often subdued or covered with a hand to prevent people from seeing inside a bodily orifice. I line up to buy some strawberries, and the guy running the stall throws me an easy "Hey, how's it going?"

I say "Gooood" in that flat matter-of-fact tone that so many people here use when they want to be friendly but not prolong the conversation. He looks at me with a slightly hurt pout, as if I'm the biggest curmudgeon he has encountered all morning for not wanting to engage in real dialogue. He doesn't know that I just got back from a place where small talk is not expected. As much as Tokyo has unwritten rules to be impeccably polite to one another at all times, California also has its own rules on how to not be too formal because it gets in the way of casual connection.

I am reminded of what Dr. Sugita said about the atmosphere holding educational power. What we see and feel around us teaches us how to behave. In Japan, there is one correct way to behave in public, so it's easy to be influenced by it and feel pressured by peers into acting like everybody else. I reflect on how hard I tried to shift my behavior to try to match the other moms around me, even though I knew I could never really blend in. I think about how N-chan emerged as the more dominant character during our time there, a sweet and obedient kid eager to learn the ways of society that were so clearly outlined for her. This was fun for a summer, but how would it impact who we are and who we become if we stayed there longer? I think about all the times I felt a bit uncomfortable in Tokyo even though it's the place where I grew up, like I couldn't be my full self because of how I was expected to look, think, and act.

On the flip side, how is living in free-form California affecting us? During a routine playdate at a park near our home, I observe one mom who seems to be having some very visible challenges regulating her mood. One minute, she's running after her kid in a game of tag; then, suddenly, she flips a switch and starts to loudly admonish him for trying to pop a piece of found candy into his mouth. "Noooo!" she screams, then starts counting loudly enough to make the whole playground turn heads. "One! Two! Three!" Her kid throws the candy toward his mom, and she yells again: "No throwing!" Then, seconds later, she's running after him again with a big smile on her face. It's confusing. I am confused, just watching the whole interaction.

In a corner of the playground, an angry dad is yelling at the ice cream truck man because his digital payment didn't go through. "I'm not paying twice! Stop asking me for my money!" he yells at the poor man, unaware that his son has stopped enjoying his ice cream sandwich.

There are also lots of chill moms and dads with reusable coffee mugs and polarized sunglasses enjoying the beautiful weather while watching their kids be kids—portraying the laid-back vibes that California is so well known for. I appreciate the range of reactions and emotions that we get to witness and experience here in the San Francisco Bay Area. I want my kids to see how there are many different kinds of people with many different interpretations of how to be in the world. But it's harder to find common ground when there are too many opposing views and ways to do things, when there's nothing to bind together such a wide array of people who live in close proximity to one another. The gap between the have's and the have not's continues to widen, and there is no obvious path forward for how to mend and heal some of the most fundamental challenges we face.

Neither environment is perfect, and where I've found the most inspiration is among people who are somewhere in between the calm orderliness of Japan and the chaotic diversity of California. Some of the best examples of parenting that I have seen in both places come from adults who are having fun while setting productive boundaries for their kids. When the kids see us having healthy fun, they start to find ways to build healthy fun into their own lives. We don't want the next generation to grow up with stressed-out parents who are disconnected from themselves, their kids, and the world around them. Parenting is hard—but it's also fun, right?

I feel this in my bones, over and over again, this tension between this being the hardest and the most fun thing I've ever done. So far, for me, being a Japanese-ish mom in America is a roller coaster of unbridled joy and teeth-gritting pain. I have never felt more accountable to myself and the choices I make. Keeping my physical body healthy isn't just for looking cute anymore—if I don't get enough sleep, I can't responsibly drive them to school; if I'm tired or in pain, I'll be cranky, and then I won't have the patience to read books to them at bedtime. Self-care is by extension how I can care for my kids. And self-reflection is how I become a better parent. I have had to unpeel layers and layers of my own shit and look them in the face in the hardest moments and ask myself convoluted questions when it feels like I really don't have the time or energy to do so (like: Do I really have the patience to not lose it at this kid who has ignored me for the hundredth time today? and Will tonight be another night of tortuous sleepless deprivation caused by unavoidable external circumstances?). But in the end, it's all worth it because N and M are bringing more warm, fuzzy loving goodness to my life than anything I ever imagined.

I believe that N and M are sacred little spirits who chose Hubby and me as their parents, and we have a responsibility to the world to give them a beautiful life. I'm not an anti-vaxxer, but when I took N to get her first set of immunization shots, I held back tears. I felt like she was being injected with human-engineered shit and this was going to take away her sacredness a little bit. She cried. N, meanwhile, is starting to become a little Yoda-like, dropping bits of wisdom that she picked up from I'm not sure where. "Hey, Mama," she says one morning as she waves a badminton racket around like a magic wand. "Protect your mind, okay?" The other day when Hubby and I were complimenting her on how good she was about cleaning up her toys that afternoon, she said quietly, "There is lots of magic in my world. The magic is in my mind and my mind is magic." "People are good for the world!" she declares one night before bed as she stands on my pillow with one arm raised up like Super Mario. "You're in my heart, and so is Papa, Malcolm, and M," N tells me one morning as we walk to school. "Everyone is in my heart."

My friend Susie once told me that having a child is like having your heart live outside of your body. I know what she means. Sometimes I look at N traipsing around the living room in her little mermaid outfit (a cotton crop top and matching miniskirt with blue and purple swirls mildly resembling algae) and it fills me with unbelievable joy. "Did you know that you are the thing I wanted the most in the world?" I tell her as I hold her close. "You are my reason for being." She quietly receives this message and the outpouring of love coming from me.

For N's fourth birthday, we take her out to lunch to eat whatever she wants. N requests that we go to a restaurant that has grilled cheese sandwiches—a sign that she is already reverting to her mostly carb-based American diet. I type "grilled cheese sandwich" into Google Maps, and we end up in an oversized booth table at Tom and Jerry's, a local bar that's known for being extremely kid-friendly. TV screens showing multiple sports games are already competing loudly for the attention of our poor ears, rendering any additional wails by unruly children unnoticeable; there is a laminated kids' menu with rocket ships, flowers, and other objects that kids like, plus a jar of broken crayons stacked next to waterproof menus. She chooses the meal and orders it herself, which makes her very proud. I have never seen so much orange on a single plate. The plate, sure enough, has a grilled cheese sandwich on it—two oversized pieces of toasted white bread with bright orange cheddar cheese oozing out of its sides, and an unrealistically giant stack of oversized stick-shaped fries, drenched in hot oil long enough to reach an eerily orange crispy appearance. We also get an order of their world-famous onion rings, which are even more giant and even more orange. N proceeds through her usual routine of pulling the two pieces of bread apart and peeling the cheesiest part of the grilled cheese sandwich off with her teeth. Should kids this age even be choosing what to eat? I wonder.

"I can do whatever I want!" N says.

I try a trick that I learned from Maki, another CB mom. Instead of bribing her with sugar or threatening to throw away her toys, I incentivize her with the promise of more joyous moments in the future if she adheres to my rules now. "If you eat your broccoli today, you can have more grilled cheese next time we go out," I say. And "If you put your shoes on now so we can leave on time, then we can come back here for another playdate some other day."

N spends a few short days at home before school starts, making displays with all her beautiful pink and purple fabrics and dolls. She goes back to her weekly toddler ballet class, which is nothing like the discipline and order that I witnessed at N's school in Japan. The kids are all wearing whatever they want, falling all over the place, tossing their hula hoops on the ground when they get bored.

N is reverting to the rogue and wild boundary-less childhood of the Western world. She starts ignoring my instructions and trying to negotiate everything, like what time she should be going to bed or whether she should wash her hands upon returning home. After a few weeks back in California, I am no longer the authority figure that I was in Japan. I am once again the unpredictable mom who resorts to bribes, tricks, and questions. I am giving her choices that she did not have when we were living in Tokyo. "Do you want to eat first or shower first?" "Would you rather put your shoes on by yourself, or should I help you?"

Why am I giving her so much power to choose? I ask myself.

I go back to my playbook of tricks that I learned from Japan. I need to make doing good deeds seem fun, the way Japanese schools do.

"Look, N!" I exclaim one day, pointing to a package on our doorstep. "It's a surprise present for you!"

She eagerly opens the box to find . . . a Swiffer WetJet!

"Ohhh!" she exclaims.

"It's purple! And look!" I push a button on the handle and *squirt*! Out comes cleaning fluid, right in front of the mop. She gets the hang of it right away, and ten minutes later, we have squeaky clean (and slightly slippery) wood floors.

The next day, I let her use the Dyson hand vacuum for the first time ever. She puts on her super-serious face as she holds the whirring machine half her size in both hands, sweeping up every stray dust bunny and morsel of food in sight.

When the novelty wears off, I come up with a new trick. I take little half-sheets of card stock and write step-by-step instructions that outline her bedtime routine (in Japanese, so she can read it), and then paste it all over the house like a little scavenger hunt. I even draw a little Anpanman on the first one.

Meanwhile, baby M is quickly evolving from infant to toddler. At first, she cries all the time. We draw Anpanman everywhere. On their little electric doodle boards. On envelopes with stray bills. On printouts of this manuscript. Seeing us draw Anpanman is one of the only things that makes M stop crying, so all of us—including Hubby and N—learn how to draw him, his round face and his round cheeks and his little cone-shaped body and cape.

Once she gains bodily autonomy, going from crawling to walking to running and jumping in the blink of an eye, M becomes bolder and more confident. We start to see who she really is, a happy-go-lucky, strong-willed, joyous spirit. She is the ultimate songstress, belting out tunes at perfect pitch like "Let It Go" in Japanese baby talk, doyo about butterflies and elephants, and some French songs that Hubby has been singing to her at night. She knows all the Anpanman theme songs by heart.

Meanwhile at home, Hubby downloads Duolingo and starts learning Japanese. Every night around 7:00 p.m., he and N sit on the brown MUJI beanbag in our living room and vocalize simple and sometimes very random Japanese phrases like "Tanaka-san wa dobutsu ga sukidesu" (Tanaka-san likes animals) to affirming *pings*! N often corrects her dad, saying, "No, that's not how you say that! It's *doubutsu*, not *dobutsu*." She sits next to him with a pencil in her hand, writing her name over and over in hiragana.

We start being more punctual than before. We refine our understanding of indoor versus outdoor and remove our shoes accordingly. We get the kids to put their laundry in the laundry basket. On good days, they set their own table and bus their own plates.

I try to do a little bit of self-care every day. If I can get in a thirty-minute workout three times a week and read a chapter a night of whatever novel is on my bedside table at the time, I count that as a big win. When I really need a boost, like after stretches of intensive solo parenting, I book a hotel room in some random town nearby, pack an overnight bag and some flip-flops in an oversized tote, plop my dog Malcolm in his carrier, get in the car, and drive away from the madness. Before I leave, I make sure the kids are fed, the laundry is done, and Hubby has a plan in place for the rest of the evening. But once I am out of the driveway, I do not look back. And then, over the course of twenty-four hours, I start to slowly feel more like myself.

In the early summer, just weeks before her fifth birthday, N graduates from CB. The pinnacle of a CB child's formative experience is sotsuenshiki, or graduation. It's a sweet and simple ceremony that takes place in front of a by-now well-known group of adults who have shepherded their toddler years along, together as a community, for the past three years. The ceremony itself is just ten minutes long. Sensei presents each kid with a day care diploma, each outgoing child reads a written speech of gratitude aloud to their parents, and then the teachers say some kind parting words to the new grads. A couple of the parents present the teachers with flowers. Then, after a short break, the kids present the grand finale: the graduation song and dance. The students prepare for this part of the ceremony for months in the schoolyard, learning the dance steps, memorizing words to a song about friendship. The dance they perform is called "Paprika." It's a hype song that was written for the Tokyo Olympics in 2020 (which ended up taking place in 2021 because of the pandemic). The original song and dance were performed by five kids who formed an impromptu group and quickly disbanded, leaving in their wake a highly replicable and catchy dance routine. At the CB graduation, a dozen Japanese-inspired American kids diligently show off the steps they learned. A couple of the younger toddlers veer off to play on the slides. In the background a dad chases a little sibling, who will be entering this community in the fall. But the most enthusiastic performer of all is Sensei. While most of the parents are videotaping the kids, I see her out of the corner of my eye, standing on the side but in front of her beloved students, dancing the Paprika with exaggerated movements and a big encouraging smile. ("I have to be the most enthusiastic dancer!" she tells me later. "That's the only way I can get everyone to do their best.")

Seeing Sensei dance her heart out at my daughter's day care graduation with these beautiful, well-behaved, happy kids, I'm reminded of what I think Japanese parenting in this modern era is all about. We can absolutely wholeheartedly support children in their growth—even children we didn't give birth to—while holding them to strict standards of responsibility and respect. We can guide our kids with both love and discipline. These values were baked into N's formative years by consistent, warm, and safe boundary-setting that Sensei and the other CB teachers provided every single day. Don't get me wrong: My kids are nowhere near perfect (whatever that means). They still have meltdowns and screaming matches and if you spend more than an hour with them, you probably wouldn't classify them as "calm." But there's something magical and unique that has manifested, here in this tiny little Japan-like enclave in America. The kids who grew up here are structured and caring *and* they are clearly unabashedly themselves, with individual expressions of needs, desires, and talents. Any one of us can choose to build an environment inspired by the values and practices of Japanese culture (or any other culture, for that matter). It just takes intentionality . . . and a whole lot of enthusiasm.

After this summer, N will attend an American public school for kindergarten, where her primary learning language will switch to English and she won't have her little Japanese-speaking gaggle of friends in her day-to-day life. We've enrolled her in a Japanese after-school program to keep up her language skills. We'll also make sure she doesn't forget the routines and rituals, like taking shoes off at the door and cleaning up after herself, continuing to build independence and autonomy within the existing structure of our family unit. We will always greet one another with welcome and love. We will keep trying our best to be early to places and events. We are making the most of the indoor-outdoor lifestyle that we have here, treasuring our relationship with the flowers in our yard and the ladybugs that land on them as much as we revere our ancient house dog, Malcolm. I hope N never gets tired of the Swiffer WetJet, but I'm already one step ahead of her: If she does, I'm planning to get her a real cotton mop and an Anpanman bucket.

BONUS MATERIAL!

30 Easy Ways to Bring Japanese Parenting Principles into Your Family

One of the best things about having kids is that you get to rewrite your own story of what family life is—even if it's really different from the family you grew up in. I just shared some traditional and nontraditional tips and anecdotes from my own invented life as a parent. While there is no one-size-fits-all solution, some of the best parts of Japanese-style parenting are easily adaptable to American family life, too. And they just might help you mitigate a little bit of the chaos that comes with raising kiddos. I hope you'll read these tips and find some that you can bring into your life without compromising your own idea of what parenting needs to look like for you.

1. GREET OTHERS PLEASANTLY AND POLITELY

In Japan, even the smallest child is greeted politely and seriously by the adults around them. When I drop off my kids at day care, their teachers always greet them with "ohayo gozaimasu." Parents also exchange the same greetings with one another. When everyone around you is saying "ohayo gozaimasu!", you quickly learn that you too should be greeting others pleasantly and politely. Whether you're entering a store or joining someone in an elevator, it's always nice to say hello—even if you think nobody will notice. Just one warm greeting can make someone's day.

2. CLEAN UP AFTER YOURSELF

A lot of parents clean up after their kids or around their kids. I get why. If kids aren't in the habit of cleaning up, it's easier and faster than trying to persuade them to do it themselves. But it's not a sustainable system because you'll get tired and the kids will start to expect it. Remember: you're their parent, not their servant! Teaching kids that they are also responsible for the well-being of their environment is a life lesson worth investing in. Play a cleanup song to make it a fun (and timed) activity or buy them a cleaning tool for a present. And not just the fake broom set that they sell on Amazon. Get them a real one! Giving a toddler a Swiffer WetJet or a dustpan can result in lots of fun—and cleaner floors.

3. ORGANIZE BOOKS BY COLOR AND TOYS BY CATEGORY

When kids see beautifully organized things, they will develop a heightened aesthetic and appreciation for beauty. It's easy for kids' books and toys to become the source of complete chaos and disorder. There are some simple ways that you can try to mitigate this. Sort books by the color of the spine and place them in a bookshelf for a natural rainbow decor. Don't worry about size—the range of thicknesses and heights will add some whimsy to the system of organization. Toys are trickier, but finding opaque boxes and organizing them by category has worked best in my home.

4. BELIEVE THAT EVERYTHING HAS A SPIRIT

If your books could speak, would they be thanking you for putting them on the shelf straight and aligned with their friends, or would they be wincing in pain because you folded their spines back too far and left them splayed out on the table? Are your clothes given room to breathe and rest in their drawers, or are they stuffed in and wrinkled, feeling crammed and unloved? These things matter, not because the things actually matter (they may or may not) but because the way you take care of your things is a reflection of how beautifully you live. When you think of the most mundane inanimate objects as spiritual entities, you will start to treat everything—and everyone—around you with more care.

5. ADDRESS ANIMALS WITH *-SAN*

Japanese children's songs and stories almost always address animals in the polite form, using the ending *-san*, which is kind of like saying Mister Elephant or Miss Bear (but without a gender designation). Fruits and vegetables are often addressed this way, too. When you speak about everyone and everything with this level of respect, it helps train us to be respectful of our things. Since animals and plants come from nature, this also helps you develop a closer relationship with other living beings.

6. THINK ABOUT EVERYONE'S FEELINGS (NOT JUST YOUR OWN)

Self-care is important—but in Japan, taking care of those around you is just as important as taking care of yourself. At Japanese schools, students role-play scenarios that put themselves in other people's shoes, which helps them develop compassion and empathy. How might an action you took make someone else feel? How can you bring someone along who doesn't agree or is feeling upset or isolated? Spending time putting yourself in someone else's shoes can go a long way toward building a community-centered, empathetic vibe no matter where you go or who you're with.

7. LEARN THE ART OF SAYING "DOUZO!"

One of the first words my second kid, M, learned to say is "Douzo!" Its closest equivalent in English is "Here you go!" But it is more than just a verbal expression attached to giving something to someone else; it's more of a feeling, an offering. My two kids often want to play with the exact same toy, and without the art of douzo, it can quickly become a grab battle. But as soon as someone prompts her with "Douzo!" M immediately goes into her polite offering mode and hands over whatever she is holding. "Douzo!" has been the magic formula to prevent my kids from fighting. Next time you're feeling a wee bit too possessive of something or want the last piece of fruit from a fruit bowl, try instead to relinquish your desire to the art of "Douzo!" and offer it willingly to somebody else.

8. ENCOURAGE AN "I CAN DO IT MYSELF!" MINDSET

One of the things that best builds confidence in kids is allowing them to do things themselves. Nothing beats a sense of autonomy and accomplishment! I know that sometimes it's just faster to do things for your toddler—like find their favorite stuffie, or put on their shoes, or make a simple snack. But the small investments of time and patience that it takes to encourage and wait for kids to complete tasks themselves will eventually pay off big-time.

9. KNOW THE DIFFERENCE BETWEEN INDOOR SHOES AND OUTDOOR SHOES

The bottom of your shoes can bring all kinds of nasty things into your home—bacteria, lead, bubble gum, dog poop. Teach your kids that yucky stuff from outside the house doesn't belong inside the house by creating a routine of taking off shoes as soon as you get home. Most Japanese homes have a genkan, or a formal entryway, where you leave your shoes before you enter. It's usually a step lower than the home itself, so that dirt from the streets does not accidentally get dragged in. You can create your own genkan area by providing a doormat, a shoe rack, or some other visible signal for people to take off their shoes as they enter. When taking off shoes at a genkan, it's customary to then line them up with the toes facing toward the door, so that they're ready to put back on when exiting the home. It's also common to provide slippers or indoor shoes, and separate slippers for bathrooms.

10. DO DAILY EXERCISES TOGETHER AS A FAMILY

Ask any Japanese person if they know what Radio Taiso is and they will say yes. At some point in their lives, whether at school or at work or in front of the TV, they would have done this set of exercises, along with all their peers. It's a combination of stretching, jumping, and other movements that loosen the joints and give you a little jolt of cardio that almost anyone—from the smallest child to the elderly—can safely do at home. The Japanese do this because it is an easy way to start the day with physical movement and group cohesion. My recommendation is that you try it at home with your kids. Like any other group exercise, whether that's Zumba or Pilates or a HIIT class, knowing that you're doing it with others can bring great joy and motivation—and what better way to start the weekend than to share joy and motivation with the entire family?

11. DON'T SLOUCH

In Japanese elementary schools, kids are often reminded to sit straight when in their classrooms. This is about more than just discipline. It's actually really bad for our bodies to slouch. It can lead to back problems, GI issues, and a host of other long-term problems. The National Institutes of Health estimates that 80 percent of people will experience back pain at some point in their lives. It's a good reminder to all of us that our spines are designed to be a certain way, and encouraging sitting and standing straight from early on will help us lead healthier lives.

12. DON'T INTERRUPT OTHER PEOPLE

One of the starkest differences in conversation styles between the Japanese and Americans is that the Japanese never interrupt other people, whereas Americans enjoy the rhythm of a continuous conversation in which one voice subsides as another chimes in. Of course, it's important to have the confidence to speak up, but not interrupting people is a great thing to practice, especially with kids who are naturally very adept at bringing the spotlight back to themselves.

13. TRY TO KEEP MELTDOWNS AT HOME

While I fully believe that kids should be their authentic selves, I also think it's important for kids to behave themselves just a little bit better when they're out in public. This is part and parcel of creating a more peaceful world; if everyone plays their part in maintaining the sanctity of shared spaces, then the shared spaces themselves will feel more peaceful. Next time your small kid starts to whine, complain, or scream in public, remind them that other people are around and may not necessarily want to experience the collateral damage of a toddler meltdown.

14. DON'T GIVE KIDS TOO MANY CHOICES

The Japanese don't always give kids choices on what to do—kids don't always know what they truly want, and besides, the day belongs to everyone, not just your tiny tyrants. Instead of saying, "What do you want to do today? Should we go to the museum, a park, or the library?," try saying, "Today, we are going to the library!" Of course, there are many situations in which it's healthy for kids to learn how to express their opinion or resist something they don't like, but it's also okay for them to be told what to do sometimes.

15. LET KIDS PLAY BY THEMSELVES

As tempting as it might be to run around with your kid who is having a great time playing on the geodesic dome structure and swings, consider the possibility that playground time can be a chance for you to kick back, relax, and not worry too much about what or how your kid is doing. They are probably fine. And you will be, too, as long as you stay off the playground equipment.

16. BE EARLY OR ON TIME

One of the hardest things about parenting is being on time. Kids don't care (or can't yet read) what time the clock says it is. They're usually focused on doing what's in front of them because they're so in the moment. But being on time is one of the most important values in Japanese culture. Trying to be on time—or better, early—saves you the stress of having someone else wait, and it shows that you honor and respect the other people involved. I always trick myself into believing that we have to be somewhere half an hour before we *actually* have to be there. This gives us enough wiggle room for tantrums, forgotten diapers and baby bottles, and spontaneous dance parties. Practice often enough, and one day, ideally, your hard work will pay off and your kids will be respectable, punctual people.

17. DO ONE THING AT A TIME, MINDFULLY AND CAREFULLY

Many people—myself included—feel like there aren't enough hours in the day. I am often running around the house holding stray baby bottles and an armful of laundry and trying to cram in a phone call while walking the dog before getting to my office. But this is not a sustainable or pleasant way to exist. For kids, being in distracted environments can lead to challenges with attention and in school. What if you try doing just one thing at a time? This type of mindful focus is at the core of Zen Buddhism, which is foundational to Japanese culture. If you can simplify the flow of your day so that you're doing one thing at a time, you might just help your kids find their center more easily when it matters most.

18. GREET YOUR FOOD

Whether that's saying "itadakimasu!" like all Japanese kids do, or "bon appétit!," or saying grace, a simple ceremony to greet your food can go a long way toward making mealtimes feel structured, fun, and important. It's also a moment to show gratitude for the fact that you can have this meal and respect for all the contributors (growers, suppliers, distributors, cooks) who went into getting this food here.

19. USE CUTE CHARACTERS TO HELP TEACH LESSONS

Princesses and superheroes aren't just great for pretend-play. They can be repurposed as useful tools for teaching some of life's most valuable lessons to our youngest citizens. We use a hand puppet that N lovingly calls Dr. Johnny to encourage her to brush her teeth, use the toilet, and finish her food. N likes Dr. Johnny because he gives her his undivided attention and has a silly voice. It is much more effective than me hovering over her with my normal mom voice. You, too, can find a favorite stuffie and make it come alive with some funny voice-overs to teach valuable life lessons.

20. REWARD GOOD BEHAVIOR WITH MORE GOOD BEHAVIOR

Instead of bribing kids with treats and toys, try bribing them with the promise of a bright future full of joy. "I know you don't want to leave this playdate, but if we leave now, we can come back another time." "I know you don't want to go to school, but if you go now, then we can do something super fun together after pick up." Notice that none of these promises are particularly earth-shattering—you're simply repurposing things that are likely to happen anyway into a rewards framework.

21. BUY CUTE LITTLE REWARDS FROM THE DOLLAR STORE

I know I just said you should motivate kids without bribes, but desperate times sometimes call for desperate measures, and at times when bribery feels necessary, it's good to be prepared. Whenever I go back to Tokyo, I always make a pit stop at the local hundred-yen store to pick up cute animal stickers, little hair ribbons, fuzzy colorful pipe cleaners, sparkly origami, and other random fun things. I keep them in a little bag in my closet and use them to motivate and bring joy to parenting moments that need extra support. If there's a Daiso near your house, that's a great place to stock up; otherwise any dollar store or Target or Ross Dress for Less will do the trick.

22. TRY EATING EVERYTHING AT LEAST ONCE (EVEN THINGS YOU THINK YOU WON'T LIKE)

Japanese kids don't always get to choose what they eat. But they're also usually not as picky as American kids—this could be because Japanese food is just better all around, but it also might be because they're firmly asked to try everything at least once. Try convincing your kids that tasting a new food is as big an adventure as going down a giant slide. And if they don't like it, you can still celebrate the fact that they tried!

23. MAKE RAINBOW-COLORED MEALS AND SNACKS

Next time you're packing a snack for your kids, look at the colors of the food. Is everything orange or yellow? Crackers, cheese, oranges, bananas? Or can you pack blueberries, strawberries, grapes, kiwis, mangoes? Rainbows make kids happy, and happy kids are more likely to eat their snacks if they are in the color of the rainbow. No, jellybeans and gummy bears of different colors do not count. When using the rainbow as your culinary guide, try to find natural food colors, but also think about the diversity of healthful textures, flavors, and ingredients that you can bring to your plate.

24. TAKE LESS THAN YOUR SHARE

Enryo is a Japanese concept that means to show restraint and not do something or take too much, out of respect for others.

When Japanese people share a meal, they always leave the last piece for someone else at the table to finish. What if, instead of competing to take the biggest piece, you see who can show the most enryo and take the smallest piece? Or, next time you're at a shared meal, you challenge your kid to take less than their share?

25. TAKE OCCASIONAL BREAKS FROM PARENTING

Whenever humanly possible, sneak some breaks into your day when you don't think about your kids and do something just for yourself. Maybe it's buying your favorite cheese from the grocery store and eating it alone when nobody else is home. Or going for a thirty-minute foot massage on your way home from drop-off. Whatever it is, if you do it for you, it counts as self-care.

26. BRING OMIYAGE TO YOUR NEXT OUTING

When you see a Japanese person, they are unlikely to embrace you in a big hug; instead, they will probably reach into their bag and hand you a present. Whether it's a delicious snack from where you came from or a small toy for your children, omiyage always delights the recipient. Plus, there is evidence that giving people gifts makes the giver happy, too! Next time you go to a gathering or come back from a trip, bring a box of cookies or some little trinkets as a way to say, "We were thinking of you" or "We appreciate you" through gifts, not just with words.

27. PRACTICE OMOTENASHI AT HOME

It's easy to let your guard down with the people closest to you and think you can be spoiled and sloppy. But what if—maybe not all the time but sometimes—you practice omotenashi at home? Maybe that means you bring your partner a cup of tea or offer your kid a foot massage. Or you pick up the toys in your kids' room and place them gently back in their place. Your family members might be your default best friends, but that doesn't mean you can be rude to them. In fact, they are the most important people in our lives, so it's important to give them extra-special care whenever you can.

28. ENJOY EVEN THE MOST MUNDANE THINGS

Take a cue from Marie Kondo and the Buddhist monks. Even simple "chores" like tidying up a drawer, washing dishes, or sweeping outside the house can bring immense joy. In a world filled with big dreams and lots of screen time (and who knows what's next?), staying connected to your physical surroundings through these analog tasks can bring immense joy. Try to slow down and do them without causing too much collateral damage—doing things mindfully and quietly can lead to an abundance of inner peace and satisfaction.

29. PRACTICE FEELING PEACEFUL

We often say Japan is a "heiwa na kuni"—a peaceful country. Heiwa, or peace, can be used to describe a person, a place, or a society. Japan was not always a peaceful country—it adopted pacifism as a core value only after its defeat in World War II. Ever since then, peace has become a core part of our national brand, and a core part of our collective identity. When being peaceful is a value that drives every person in society, the whole society feels pretty peaceful, too. The trick to showing kids how to be peaceful is to find your own peace first. This is harder than it sounds, but the more you practice, the easier it will become and the more peaceful your family will be, along with your surroundings.

30. KEEP YOUR MIND AND YOUR INTENTIONS PURE

Keeping your mind and intentions pure is an important aspect of being parents and guardians of little ones who are just learning about the world. Human minds are very powerful, but most adults have stubborn habits that are hard to break. Kids, on the other hand, are like sponges, ready and able to soak up almost anything. And they're intuitive, too—they can always sense when something is off. You owe it to your kiddos to keep what you transmit into their surroundings as clean as possible, so that you don't introduce unintended complexity into their lives.

How to Prepare an Awesome Mom Bag

In Chapter 4, I share the story of a trip my family took down the Pacific Coast, where I discover how a Japanese mom friend of mine keeps all her kid things perfectly organized during multi-hour outings. Here are some simple steps you can follow to create your own version of Satomi's amazing mom bag.

First, find a bag that's big but not unwieldy, that is easy to carry around. A large boxy backpack is great, but if like me you're happier slinging a bag over your shoulder, find a tote that keeps its shape and doesn't become a bottomless pit. Then, find five smaller pouches that will fit inside the bag neatly together, and fill them as follows:

POUCH 1: SNACKS

- Dry snacks like popcorn and bunny crackers, placed in reusable snack cups
- Fruits and cheese, cut up and placed in little well-sealed bento boxes (If it's hot outside, pack it next to a small ice pack.)
- Fruit-and-vegetable juice pouches for an instant hit of nutrition and energy

POUCH 2: KITCHENWARE

- A couple of reusable bendy silicone straws, ideally in rainbow colors
- Kids' forks and spoons and chopsticks
- Bibs for messy eaters
- Scissors for cutting meats and vegetables at restaurants into kid sizes (This is much more efficient and safer than a fork and knife.)
- A small packet of hand wipes and/or hand sanitizer

POUCH 3: TOILETRY ITEMS

- Diapers/undies
- A compact pack of wipes
- Cute, oversized toilet seat covers

POUCH 4: TOYS

- Small notebooks
- Coloring pages (There are many websites where you can print these for free.)
- Origami
- Little crayons that don't stain

POUCH 5: CHANGE OF CLOTHES

- Extra pants, socks, and a shirt for each kid (Nothing too bulky!)
- A small towel for spills and accidents

SIDE / FRONT POCKET OF BACKPACK OR TOTE:

- Wet wipes, useful for everything
- Water bottles

Important: Make sure you refill your mom bag pouches every time you return from an outing. Wash the cutlery, bibs, and other used items. Like everything else, pack the items in the pouches and the pouches in the larger bag with care, so that everything stays very neat, organized, and easy to access.

How to Make a Very Basic "Kawaii" Toddler-Friendly Bento Box

In Chapter 6, I write about how one of the keystone elements of a Japanese-inspired childhood is the bento—a thoughtfully prepared, handmade lunch that says "I love you" without using words. With a little bit of effort and creativity, you too can design your own Japanese-inspired bento box that will make your kid squeal with delight and eat more types of food. Remember: A good Japanese bento is a balance between love, cuteness, nutrition, and design. Bonus points if you engage your child in creating the bento! (But no pressure!)

INGREDIENTS

ONIGIRI:

- Cooked short-grain Japanese white rice, still warm and placed in a medium-sized bowl
- Unflavored seaweed, cut into approximately 2 × 4-inch (5 × 10-cm) strips
- Condiments to put in the middle. Try umeboshi, tuna salad, natto, salmon, kombu—whatever you like!

PROTEIN:

- Cooked salmon, chicken nuggets, a cube of cheddar cheese, a cut-up meatball—anything!

COLORFUL VEGGIE SIDES:

- Cooked carrots
- Cucumbers
- Baby tomatoes

Pro tip: Fruits are also great! Think vitamins, minerals, and lots of colors.

TOOLS

- Bento box
- Clean hands
- Small dipping bowl filled with warm water
- Rice scooper or large spoon
- Small cookie cutters (optional, for shaping veggies)

INSTRUCTIONS:

1. Stage all the ingredients so they're easily within reach.
2. Dip clean hands in the small water bowl. This prevents the rice from sticking to your hands.
3. Take a golf-ball-sized portion of rice from the bowl and pat it into a round shape with your hands. If you want to put a condiment in the middle, stick your finger in the middle of the rice ball and place a tiny bit of your condiment in the center, then wrap the rice back around so that it is held in place.
4. Once you're satisfied with the shape, wrap the seaweed across the center of the rice ball like a bellyband.
5. Cut the veggie sides into small bite-sized portions, using the cookie cutters to make fun shapes.

Place the onigiri and sides neatly in the bento box. Let cool before closing the lid.

ACKNOWLEDGMENTS

This book would not have been possible without the collective wisdom and support of so many people.

Thank you to . . .

. . . The amazing subject matter experts who shared their insights with me: Fumino Sugiyama, Dr. Hiroshi Sugita, Joi Ito, Chiyo Takahashi, Ema Ryan Yamazaki, Matt Alt, Mayumi Uejima-Carr, Dr. Oliver Curry, Sarah Birke, Dr. Siggie Cohen, the team at Pigeon PR. Your insights and expertise transformed this book from a floaty memoir to something more substantial and universal.

. . . The Japanese and Japanese-inspired moms and dads and caregivers who agreed to speak with me in confidence about your experience of loving and raising your children in today's evolving parenting landscape, both in Japan and in the United States.

. . . The CB mama crew, for sharing this journey of raising Japanese-inspired toddlers with me. Many of you shared your perspectives and stories. Some of you generously took the time to read excerpts from early drafts, making sure I was not misrepresenting our little community. As I write in Chapter 3, I believe that who our "mom friends" are matters, because we end up spending a lot of time together, whether we like it or not. I'm grateful that I get to be with you all while our kids go through their toddler days.

. . . The teachers at CB and the many other caregivers, teachers, and learning specialists who are helping to raise my kids. It truly takes a village. I am so grateful for the non-judgmental, all-around positive vibes that you all have instilled in our children. They are so happy and confident, and I know it's because they spend so many special moments with you. And really, this shout-out expands out to all the incredible educators and care providers who support families and children, all over the world. I don't know how you do it, day in and day out.

. . . The publishing industry magic-makers who participated in making this book project come to life. Rebecca Smith-Hurd helped tighten up my early proposal so that it was clear and compelling enough to shop around. My agent, Rica Allanic at the David Black Agency, whose superpowers include honesty, kindness, and efficiency, gave me the early feedback that helped refine the vision and marketability of this book. The editorial, design, and marketing experts at Workman have been great partners in transforming this book from a fun concept to something that now stands on its own feet. My inimitable editor Maisie Tivnan brought her joyful energy and deep expertise of the world of parenting books to this project, and Analucia Zepeda deftly jumped in to tie up loose ends and bring it to the finish line. Shout-out to artist Saori Wago for the cute cover illo!

. . . My parents, my brother, and my nephew in Tokyo for the countless hours you've spent entertaining, feeding, and being present with my kids, in Japan and beyond.

. . . Annie and Uncle Rick, for all the Christmas trees and birthday songs and FaceTime stories and toddler chit-chat.

. . . Masa-san, Aunt Ji Li, JoyJoy, Gray, and the rest of the extended family—for spending extra time with our kids and for making the fabric of our lives so colorful and fun.

. . . My amazing lifelong friends from all over the world who have been by my side from when parenthood was an abstract, far-in-the-future idea.

. . . Hubby, for copiloting this wild adventure and for the unconditional love you pour into this family.

It may not be very Japanese of me to say this so directly, but I love you all very much.

. . . N and M. You two are my light, my reason for being, my greatest source of joy and resilience. Nobody could have ever preempted for me what parenting is really like. Like the physical pain of birthing children, it's literally impossible to describe in words. In the context of this being the gratitude-sharing section for this book, obviously without you two I would have never become a parent, and without that I would not have written this book. I have infinite love and gratitude for you both, always.

This book is dedicated to Malcolm, my ancient dog. He has been by my side since 2008. Everyone is always surprised that he is still here, but as this book goes to print, he is lying next to me on a retired infant Boppy pillow, sleeping soundly and peacefully. When raising children feels too hard, it's Malcolm who comes to my rescue simply by being himself.

Lisa Katayama is a working mom and writer who was born and raised in Tokyo. She is the author of two books, including *Urawaza: Secret Everyday Tips and Tricks from Japan*, and is a former tech and culture journalist for *Wired*, *Fast Company*, and *The New York Times Magazine*. Katayama is a US-Japan Leadership Program Fellow and an Asia Society Young Leader and was named one of Forbes Japan's Top Women to Watch in 2018. She currently serves as Chief Transformation Officer for the Japanese technology company Digital Garage and lives in Northern California with her family.

RAISING READERS

Books Build Bright Futures

Thank you for reading this book and for being a reader of books in general. We are so grateful to share being part of a community of readers with you, and we hope you will join us in passing our love of books on to the next generation of readers.

Did you know that reading for enjoyment is the single biggest predictor of a child's future happiness and success?

More than family circumstances, parents' educational background, or income, reading impacts a child's future academic performance, emotional well-being, communication skills, economic security, ambition, and happiness.

Studies show that kids reading for enjoyment in the US is in rapid decline:

- In 2012, 53% of 9-year-olds read almost every day. Just 10 years later, in 2022, the number had fallen to 39%.
- In 2012, 27% of 13-year-olds read for fun daily. By 2023, that number was just 14%.

Together, we can commit to **Raising Readers** and change this trend. How?

- Read to children in your life daily.
- Model reading as a fun activity.
- Reduce screen time.
- Start a family, school, or community book club.
- Visit bookstores and libraries regularly.
- Listen to audiobooks.
- Read the book before you see the movie.
- Encourage your child to read aloud to a pet or stuffed animal.
- Give books as gifts.
- Donate books to families and communities in need.

BOB1217

Books build bright futures, and **Raising Readers** is our shared responsibility.

For more information, visit **JoinRaisingReaders.com**

Sources: National Endowment for the Arts, National Assessment of Educational Progress, WorldBookDay.com, Nielsen BookData's 2023 "Understanding the Children's Book Consumer"